Freeing the Truth

Freeing the Truth

BERNARD O'CONNOR

StoryTerrace

CONTENTS

INTRODUCTION

I wish to dedicate this book to all the members of my family who experienced at first hand the events mentioned in this book and had to, as a result, live with the psychological effects and personal trauma imposed upon them by the agents of peace and justice throughout their lives.

As the author of this book, I tried to bring to the readers my vast experience as an educator, having been part of the education system as a teacher and a school principal for forty years; as a youth leader and founder of the Catholic Boy Scouts of Ireland/Scouting Ireland in Fermanagh since 1962; as a psychotherapist for the past 20 years; as a dedicated and committed member of the GAA; and most importantly as a co-parent of eight wonderful children.

My life experiences have been so traumatic, eventful, and despite all I was put through, successful, that I felt it important to put them all in print while I am still above the sod.

In writing this book I wish to acknowledge the support and help I received from my wife, Roisin, whose nimble fingers and speed on the keyboard made sure this book got produced. I am deeply indebted to my legal team of Tony

McGettigan, Eleanor Morris, Senior Council Charles Hill and James Brady.

I received life-long support in Scouting from a magnificent team of fantastic Scout Leaders, but, in particular, I must thank the late Brendan Conway(RIP), Tommy Quinn and Christine Gormley at local level and the late Michael O'Driscoll(RIP), Gerry Moan, Pat Hollinsworth, Paul Ring, and Joe Lawlor at National Level. It would be remiss of me not to mention the loyal support I got from Brother Aloysius and Brother Peter in St Michael's Primary School and Hannah McCusker, Brian Treacy and the most energetic secretary, Mary Hallett, in St Patrick's Primary School, Mullanaskea. During my 20 years with Accord, I was wonderfully supported by three most dedicated ladies, Donna McAuliffe, Breda O'Hanrahan(RIP) and secretary Margaret Molloy.

In particular, I am deeply indebted to the BBC for bringing my experiences to the attention of the nation despite serious political pressure. The producer of the Tonight BBC TV Programme, Janine Thomason(RIP) and interviewer Keith Kyle(RIP) were professionally empathic in making sure that my story was allowed to be told factually and with conviction.

Finally, but most importantly, I most sincerely thank Felicity McCall, my ghost writer, for all her expertise in helping me to write this book. Her support, advice and guidance has been invaluable as well as her ability to put my story on paper. Without her, this project would have never reached fruition. I also wish to thank the editor, Martin Whittemore, and his editorial team from Story Terrace for all their guidance and professional help in getting this book published.

It is possible that some readers of this book could be hurt by what I have written. That is not my intention. The main purpose in writing this book is to expose a system of torture which was orchestrated to take over the mind of those being abused in order to extract confessions to crimes that they never committed. This was the case of the Birmingham Six and the Guilford Four and many more throughout the North of Ireland.

1

A FERMANAGH CHILDHOOD

I was born on 21st June 1942, in the townland of Silverhill near Enniskillen. My father, Phil, was working at the US base in St Angelo, managing the licensed trade and food supplies for the troops. That was his background – he had grown up in the town of Arva, in Co. Cavan, where his father, Bernard, had been a pillar of the business community. Arva is a small, thriving town where three counties and three Provinces meet – Connacht, Leinster and Ulster – and Bernard operated many businesses. As well as the licensed trade, he ran a grocery, a grain store, a bakery and an undertaker. He also had a responsibility for issuing gun licences. He was active across every aspect of community life there and was effectively the Lord of the Manor.

But all this was to go badly wrong. My grandfather ran the businesses into the ground so that, when he died, he left a legacy of debt. Phil, as the eldest, had no option but to go to England to seek work, sending money home to try to salvage the family business – not easy during war time. It was there that he met my mother, Kathleen Hand, who came from a farming background in Scotshouse, Co. Monaghan. Their divergent backgrounds were to be a source of occasional conflict in the years ahead. They were united in being hard workers, avid Fianna Fail supporters and devout Catholics. Through sheer effort and dedication, my father succeeded in rescuing the family business in Arva for his mother and siblings and in due course, he and Kathleen were married. In time, they returned to Ireland with my sister, Kathleen, who's a year older than myself, and settled in Silverhill. I was a war baby and well remember growing up with the rituals and restrictions of ration books and clothing coupons.

My father took on the management of a pub at the bottom of Queen Street, in Enniskillen, the Lower House, and we moved to live over the premises. They were next door to the RUC Police Station and training depot for all recruits to the RUC – an interesting juxtaposition!

The pub was my father's passion. He lived for it, and he gave his all to it. My mother never liked the pub business. She saw it as facilitating men who stayed out late drinking when they should have been at home with their families. Although not teetotal, she had no love of alcohol and never drank anything more than an occasional sherry. Closing time existed only in theory – such is the nature of a community pub. Being next door to the police station, it wasn't unusual for three or four officers to come in, allegedly to enforce the law, and end up drinking till three or four in the morning.

How could my father refuse to serve them? Similarly, while Sunday opening was illegal, it was common to get a knock at the door from a customer looking for a Sunday morning cure. My mother would never open the door to such callers. If there was trouble with customers, caused by too much drink, my mother would embark on one of her unsuccessful campaigns to persuade my father to give up the licensed trade and invest in farmland. Her own background was in farming, and she felt it was more wholesome and conducive to family life.

Every six months, 200 new recruits would arrive at the RUC training centre and in this period of relative stability in the north, relations were generally amicable. The front gate to the police station was always wide open. The alley between the pub and the police station was where up to 50 young lads would gather after school to play football. Police officers would often act as referees for impromptu matches. Our gable wall was where the local boys played handball. Any stray balls going over the barrack wall were quickly returned – or we were welcome to go and retrieve them. This was my world, and it was a happy one. Only with the emergence of the IRA's border campaign in 1956 would we see relationships change forever.

Radio Eireann played an integral part in my childhood. It was the constant background of sound. *The Kennedys... Dear Frankie...Ceili House...* our whole schedule revolved around the radio. As a family we were football fanatics.

The battery radio sat on its shelf and you could have heard a pin drop during games. No one spoke, no one left the room, no one moved in case we knocked the radio off the signal and lost a single word of Michael O'Hehir's animated commentary. I remember the All-Ireland Final between Cavan and Kerry at 10p.m. My father was of course a Cavan supporter and on match days the blue and white flag would flutter outside the window. My mother remained staunchly loyal to her native Monaghan. On one occasion it was definitely a house of divided loyalties as Cavan faced Monaghan in the Ulster Final at Breffni Park. It should of course have been played in Clones, but Cavan protested this would give Monaghan an unfair home advantage and won their case to have the game relocated. Cavan secured the victory and my parents didn't speak for a week! On another occasion, we travelled by train to watch an Ulster final of Armagh vs Cavan at Clones. I recall a youngster in the crowd being intrigued by the Mna and Fir signs and asking his father where the people were going. The rejoinder? "You know the wee shed in our garden, son? Well, that's what that is." This, from a man who quite casually told us his hometown was "Porty-f******down!" So much for Armagh supporters. Needless to say, Cavan won the day and we returned home triumphant.

My mother was a very devout woman. It was Mass every day during Lent before school and Devotions every night. The Rosary was said nightly. First Fridays were observed and there were religious artefacts throughout the house. With regards to Sundays, it was always Mass of course. Every Sunday the young recruits from the police training depot would parade from there to either Mass or church, and a small number of them, no more than five or six, would break off from the main bunch and go into Mass. One of them was to become internationally acclaimed as the tenor Josef Locke, serving in the force under his birth name of Joe McLaughlin from Derry. In the afternoons the same group would go for a run out in the road. They also did baton drill on the square in front of the police station to Sousa marches. It was great to watch them from my bedroom window.

On Sunday evenings we would walk three miles to the Graan Monastery for Devotions. Fr Brian D'Arcy was one of the student priests there on the altar. We went to that Monastery for Novenas and May processions. They always had great preachers. If we did not go to the Graan on an odd Sunday we went on the back of our parents' bicycles to visit houses out in the country, especially in the summer. The houses we visited were the Kinnaghans, Lizzy McConnell's and Sandy McConnell's in Bellanaleck. I particularly liked going to the Kinnaghan family because the boys were great footballers and really nice people. Sandy McConnell's family were the famous musical family – Michael and Cormac.

The intensity of my mother's religious practice never deterred me from my own faith and throughout my education, my experience of the religious orders was always positive, although some teachers could be strict. I always felt very safe in their care.

Mondays were special as my father closed the pub on Monday afternoons. He was so preoccupied with business that it was only in my late teens and twenties that we began to develop a closer relationship, but Mondays had always been special for us. On that day he would take me out in a rowing boat on the river and we would go fishing. It was wonderful to spend time together like that.

My mother was an amazingly strong woman who did everything for herself including painting and wallpapering; there was never a need for a tradesman. On Saturdays, my sister and I had our allotted chores. Mine included cleaning the linoleum from the front door to the back, and polishing all my mother's cherished brasses – she loved antiques – before I could even think about escaping to my beloved football. The abiding aromas of my childhood days are Mansion polish and Brasso!

I learned to cook, to bake apple pies and Christmas cakes. She made me self-sufficient, unusual perhaps for sons in those times. We were surprised and delighted with the arrival of my second sister, Petronella, when I was 14. We took turns at rocking an often-restless baby to sleep. Such was my naivete that I had only last minute noticed my mother spending more time in bed and avoiding going out; when I was told she had gone to the hospital and we would have a new baby, I truly thought someone would give the baby to her there. But it was great: the family adored our new addition after so long an interval, and in later years Petronella would prove to be my mother's salvation.

My education began at Abbey Street Junior School, which I attended for two years before I enrolled at St Michael's with the Presentation Brothers. At Abbey Street, I remember being taught by Sister John Bosco, the loveliest looking woman I have ever met with a personality to match. She was a saint. Mother Paula was of a different ilk. She couldn't tolerate me being a left hander. Eventually, desperate measures were called for. She removed a safety pin from beneath her robes and pinned the left sleeve of my beautiful bright green jumper that my mother, an expert knitter, had crafted for me, to its chest, to restrain the left arm. Frustrated at trying to write with my right hand, I ripped out the pin, making a big hole in my jumper in the process. I got into trouble for that when I went home, as to my mother the religious could do no wrong. As a result of this I became ambidextrous and remain so to this day.

This was to be the pattern for my schooldays; if I was in trouble at school, I was in trouble at home, as my mother would always take the side of the religious orders teaching me. A massively proud woman, she saw this as me letting her down. "The whole town is talking about you," was a refrain that would resonate with me long after my schooldays ended. When I was about 14, I wanted to play football all the time. However, when my Christmas report came from school, I was placed 32nd out of a class of 36. My mother took my good Blackthorn football boots and lifted the ring of the range and in went both my boots and my football gear. I really hated her for doing that to me at the time and I was not allowed to play football until my summer school report came out the following May. In hindsight, it was the best lesson I was ever taught, and it eventually enabled me to get my priorities right.

A similar issue for me was my piano lessons. I was sent to a music tutor at nine years of age to learn the piano. The music tutor was a woman of over 50 and her mother was in her 80s. When I would ring her doorbell, it would take the old mother a long time to answer the door so I would ring it again in case she did not hear it. When the old lady would eventually answer the door, she would greet me with an accusation that I had no manners ringing her doorbell twice. The music lesson was good, provided I did not make a mistake. The punishment for a wrong note was a whack with a long knitting needle on the back of my hand. I tried to convince my mother that I would not go back but my mother would not give in. In fact, it meant that she insisted on me doing a lot more practice on the piano upstairs and that would mean that I would not get the knitting needle. Again, in hindsight, my piano playing helped me during my time in the training college as music turned out to be one of my top subjects and played a big part in my teaching career.

From St Michael's Primary I continued to St Michael's College, where we were the first class to enter that new complex at Drumclay. One of the most notable pupils in that class was Peter Quinn, ex GAA President and brother of the famous entrepreneur Sean Quinn. Peter was a brilliant student and a genuinely lovely young person to know. However, on the football field he would let you know he was there!

During the long summer holidays from school, I would spend at least a month at my mother's home farm in Scotshouse. I loved going there as my uncles were football fanatics and excellent farmers. We played every match over and over again. They'd also let me drive tractors, make hay, cut turf and have a bucket between my legs milking a cow. When football matches were in Croke Park, my uncles would bring me to them. I remember my Uncle Benny carrying me on his shoulders into my first All-Ireland Final between Derry and Dublin in 1957. Those were great experiences.

In my teenage years I was blessed to have an excellent group of peers in Queen Street. Austin Sheerin's mother mothered us all. We congregated in her house as our social centre. She was a semi-invalid who loved our company. We listened to country and western music, showband music and Irish dance music as well as enjoying card playing and board games. We spent hours in that house singing and Irish dancing. She loved to hear our stories about the ceili dances we went to, as well as showband dances. When I would go missing, I was sure to be found in Sheerins. On the darker side, we were brought to a juvenile court because we entered a derelict sawmill and took handfuls of steeples to use in our elastic band catapults to fire at pigeons. Although a very trivial and minor offence, I was reminded of it later in life by the RUC.

Ours was an intensely political house. Both my parents were ardent Fianna Fail supporters with a huge loyalty to De Valera. The Irish Press was the only daily newspaper that came into our house. One day I went to Donnelly's Newsagent to get the Irish Press. There were no Irish Press newspapers left but the newsagent sold me the Irish Independent instead. He told me it was the same as the other Dublin newspaper. When I arrived home and gave it to my mother, she gave out to me for bringing "That blue shirt rag" into the house and it went into the range where my football gear went.

I recall when I was eight or nine years old, Dev was scheduled to open the Feis in Newtownbutler, at the invitation of the local PP Fr Tom McGuire, an out-and-out rebel. We were taken to see this momentous occasion. On the day of the opening parade, Fr Tom proudly flew a Tricolor out of the window of his house on Main Street. The police duly arrived with ladders to remove it and there followed a pantomime, with the flag been withdrawn when the police appeared and thrust out again as they withdrew. But things would shortly take a much darker turn when the police attacked the Feis parade with water cannons. People could not believe it. No one had seen it coming. The mood was beginning to change.

The IRA's 1956 border campaign and the raid on Omagh police station would further polarise opinion. We listened intently to the coverage on RTE news – the only news ever listened to in our house. One of the men arrested in the campaign, Philip Clarke, was put up as a Sinn Fein candidate in the forthcoming Fermanagh South Tyrone by-election. Campaigning was hands-on with trailers in the street and prominent figures like Rory O'Bradaigh using loudspeakers to rally public opinion. The nationalist community responded with enthusiasm; it was a case of "stand up and be counted." Later, when Cathar Healey won the seat for the Nationalist party and organised a victory parade through the town, we were kept upstairs at home. My father had a forewarning of trouble. We bottled our own Guinness out the back of the pub and before the parade began, supporters were seen coming out from behind the premises with sacks full of empty bottles. It would have been forbidden to carry a Tricolor during the parade, so instead the organisers carried three massive flags – one green, one white and one orange – the components of the Tricolor. As the police moved in to remove them, a massive riot ensued in Darling Street. Walking there the next day, we found ourselves ankle deep in broken glass. The bottles had been used to attack the police; the police had attacked the marchers. It had been an open and violent confrontation. There was a great upsurge of solidarity among the nationalist community in the aftermath. There were no longer any grey areas. Everything was black and white. It was a foretaste of the mood in the constituency some 20 years later when the hunger striker Bobby Sands would contest and win the Westminster seat. The electoral process had become a straight sectarian headcount. Things were forever changed from the days when the local police refereed our football matches and left the barrack gates open for us to come and go.

I was to experience blatant sectarianism myself when I left school at 18 after my Senior Certificate. I had at one stage considered a vocation although, perhaps surprisingly, my mother did not actively encourage this: rather, she urged me to seek a permanent, pensionable position, one with all the security sadly lacking from the licensed trade. I applied to become a technician with British Telecom and sailed through the interviews, only to be turned down on a sectarian issue. It was my first adult experience of blatant discrimination, and it rankled.

Next, I applied for and was accepted by the Inland Revenue where I worked for two years. It was while I was working there that I met up with Brother Adrian, from my primary school days. He told me, "You have the makings of a good teacher." That was my turning point. I applied for St Joseph's Training College in Belfast and, while I was waiting to start my course, in the autumn of 1962, he arranged for me to work in my old school in a temporary capacity. I loved it. This confirmed I was now set on my career path for life.

It was in the May at the end of that first year that family life changed forever. Fr McAnaney, the Dean of the College, sent for me to tell me the news that my father was "not too well." He personally drove me to the Erne hospital in Enniskillen where we found him sleeping. He had suffered a brain haemorrhage. I kept a vigil for two days, during which my father slept, slipping in and out of consciousness, though we were told his condition had stabilised. He was heavily sedated. Again, Fr McAnaney offered a lifeline. He knew a brain surgeon at the Royal Victoria Hospital, Colin Gledhill, who, for a fee of £50, agreed to travel to the Erne to examine my father. Mr Gledhill then undertook to move my father to the Royal where he believed he could carry out an operation to relieve the pressure on the brain. However, once he began the surgery, it became clear that the damage was irreversible and that my father had suffered a second haemorrhage. It was just a matter of time. It was the toughest thing I had ever had to face; it was really, really hard. My father was dying and there was nothing I could do. It was all the more painful because in recent years we had begun to form a very strong bond. During my childhood the pressure of work had made my father a rather distant figure – apart from those cherished Monday trips on the river. All his energy had gone into making a success of the pub. But now he had been coming to see me play for Enniskillen Gaels and we had begun to have long father-son conversations, to really share things, to get to know each other. Now, at just 57 years of age, he was gone.

My mother's strength saw her through. We had the inevitable conversation: would we keep the pub, with me returning home to manage it, or would I continue with my teacher training? She was relieved when I said I would prefer to remain at college. The pub went, my mother moved house and the premises eventually went to slum clearance as the road was widened. All structural vestiges of my childhood are now gone forever.

Petronella, then just six, was to be my mother's salvation. They grew closer and closer and apart from attending Queen's University to study for her music degree, Petronella never left my mother. She lived at home and taught music at St Comhgall's Secondary School, Lisnaskea. She never married. They were like sisters and remained so until my mother's death at the age of 94, after half a century of widowhood.

I returned to St Joseph's for my second-year teacher training, although I came home to Enniskillen every weekend, partly to support my mother and sister. I had now moved out of halls and was lodging with Mrs Boyle at Gransha Parade off the Glen Road. In many ways I had an advantage over my fellow students, being 21 with two years' work experience behind me. I had no difficulty in making my grant last for the duration of the term, my budgeting helped by the fact I neither smoked nor drank. I made many marvellous friends at college; I think my comparative maturity meant they tended to look up to me. Also, I had already had the experience of hands-on teaching and had no doubt that this was my vocation, whereas for some of them it had yet to be tried and proven as a career path. There were lads there who had come straight from boarding school with little experience of the wider world. I can still recall one unfortunate student who lost his entire grant gambling within the first weeks of term. Such naivete was pitiful.

We were blessed with marvellous lecturers. Two stand out in my memory. One was Seamus Heaney, a very gentle soul, with a lovely smile, so persuasive in getting us to work for him. What an honour to have been among the first students in his English classes. The other was Jim McKeever who taught PE. As the midfielder in the Derry team I'd watched him play at Croke Park from the grandstand view of my uncle's shoulders, so he had long been an idol of mine. Dr Rogers, the College President, was a legend, with the students very much in awe of him. One of our duties was to serve him 7 a.m. Mass for a week on a rota basis. If a student was late, he had to serve for a second week. This happened to an unfortunate neighbour of mine. I recall being wakened by the sound of Dr Rogers thumping on his bedroom door, shouting at him to "get up, get up!" Needless to say, he ended up serving for a fortnight.

Extracurricular activities abounded. I played for the College football team in the Antrim League and inter-college games which ensured that when I returned home at weekends to play for Enniskillen Gaels, I was super fit. My early piano lessons stood me in good stead, as did my years in the parish and school choirs, for I excelled at music and played a prominent role in the College's drama club. We staged one or two productions every year. Most memorable was our production of *Juno and the Paycock* where I was cast in the lead role of Juno. We entered it in the Belfast Festival and I proudly took home the gold medal for best actor. As a result, I was offered a career on the boards, which I declined.

Back in Enniskillen at weekends, I was active in the local operatic society, rehearsing for the latest Gilbert and Sullivan production. My early teaching practice took me to schools across Belfast – Antrim Road, Oxford Street, Ballyhackamore – giving me a great understanding of the wider Belfast community and always in apprehension of the visit from one of our lecturers for assessment. I must have acquitted myself well as I obtained a grade A certificate. For my final year, extended teaching practice, I would return home to Enniskillen, a decision which was to irrevocably change the course of my future.

I found Belfast a very unique city. In my spare time as a student, I used to love heading down to the Old Smithfield market area, where I loved to mooch around all the second-hand stuff and acquire many sporting, musical and educational artefacts and books. A number of us would go down to see the soccer internationals in Windsor Park where we witnessed the great skills of George Best and listened to the sectarian abuse given to Pat Jennings.

I also recall an infamous Sunday afternoon when I got an early lift back from Enniskillen. Two other students and I, with time on our hands, challenged each other to go to the Ulster Hall to witness the now famous Ian Paisley. He was a very controversial figure at this time. We tidied ourselves up and boarded a double decker to the city centre. On entering the Ulster Hall, we were cordially greeted as loyal brethren and furnished with hymn books and other literature. Paisley had a strong, forceful, powerful demeanour, with jet black, well-groomed hair. With well-orchestrated tonal changes to his voice, he preached a very long sermon on how the Pope was an anti-Christ and he quoted scripture from the Bible to prove his theory. It was so powerful that we sat like scared rats, afraid to even look at each other. We were so glad to escape back to College when it was all over. When we returned the other students were arriving back from all over the north, so the three of us got up on chairs in the TV room and put on the Paisley Show. We had the place in stitches. However, word got to the Dean of the College and we were summoned to his room after eleven o'clock that night. We got a severe lecture from him and he sent a letter to all of our parents. You can guess what reception I got when I went home the following weekend!

I had been involved with the junior Legion of Mary in Enniskillen and it was only natural that I would engage with the organisation proper in Belfast, joining the branch based at the College. I was one of a number of students selected each year to work with youth groups including Nazareth Lodge and Ormeau Road. I marvelled at the commitment of the young boxers we encountered, putting in hours of training in what can only be described as horrible conditions. Their Olympic medals were testament to their dedication, and well deserved. In another area, St Augustine's in Great Victoria Street, the parish priest, Fr Kennedy, involved us in working with the youths from Kircubbin Remand Home. Many children had family support – though there were others who had no family support – but they were still years behind educationally and efforts had to be made to secure apprenticeships and employment for them when they left the home. We taught them basic maths, measuring, spelling – it was teaching in a very, very different environment, and, as such, rewarding. Fr Kennedy had recruited a team of young women volunteers – civil servants and teachers – who plied us with tea and sandwiches at these sessions. It was here that my friend and fellow student Denis Ward and I came to meet Maura and Patricia. Patricia Crosbie was a civil servant whose family hailed from Haypark Avenue in the Ormeau Road. The four of us became firm friends, then romance blossomed. Denis would marry Maura and together they would move to his native County Down when he took up a teaching post in Newry.

From the start, I was welcomed into Patricia's family – indeed, I was made to feel like a God! The reaction from my own mother was less supportive. It's hard to rationalise this as she had no personal objection to Patricia; how could she dislike this lovely, respectable young woman? Rather it was a pattern that had evidenced itself when I had my first girlfriend whilst I was a teenager studying in the Gaeltacht. My mother objected to her and worked to break up the relationship. Later, she went to unbelievable lengths to break up my five-year relationship with a lovely girl from Maguiresbridge. I can only explain it by saying it was nothing personal against the girls. It was simply that no woman would ever be good enough for her son. As the time approached for me to go home to do my extended teaching practice, Patricia and her family were concerned my mother would seize the opportunity to try to break us up and were determined that history would not repeat itself. We were married in Belfast on 28th December 1965, before it began. Various members of the clergy, and others, tried to intervene on both our behalf, but my mother and my sister refused to attend the wedding. I did, however, have family support from my father's sister and my mother's brothers and their wives, so I was not totally alone. Afterwards, I commuted to Enniskillen on a daily basis, returning to my "home from home" with Patricia's family every night.

I had no difficulty securing my first teaching job. I knew there was one, possibly two, vacancies coming up in my old school, St Michael's, and one of them was mine. I was to remain on the staff there for 21 years. I didn't even have to do an interview.

In my teaching career in St Michael's Primary School, I enjoyed many outstanding experiences between 1966 and 1986. I was so fortunate to have worked under an outstanding principal, Bro Aloysius, and a wonderful team of teachers including my own first teacher, Sr John Bosco. As a staff we had a serious setback when Mrs McMahon's husband John and her two children were killed when their aeroplane crashed into a mountain outside Enniskillen on their way to see Pope John in Galway. On a lighter note, I also recall a visit from Fr Finnegan to my P4 class. He was the religious examiner at the time and during his questioning of my class he asked a boy, "Who was the mother of John the Baptist?" The wee lad enthusiastically replied, "Queen Elizabeth!"

I eventually became one of the teachers for the 11 Plus exam class where year on year we had record results. We also became the top school in hurling and football in Fermanagh on many occasions, as well as being Fermanagh large schools swimming champions seven years in a row. I also succeeded in training our school choir to constantly win at the Fermanagh Feis.

Once I was appointed to the staff, Patricia and I moved

to Enniskillen, to a house at 72B Derrin Park, and I began teaching in the autumn term of 1966. Our first child, Philip, was born that October, the 4th. We subsequently had seven more children – six girls and another son: Nuala 3rd June 1968; Maire 18th July 1969; Sinead 27th November 1970; Brian 15th February 1972; Aine 13th June 1975; Nollaig 31st December 1976 and Meabh 7th April 1980.

Clearly our home in Derrin Park could not contain our expanding brood, so we applied for a council house, coming up against the gerrymandering and discrimination that was prevalent in their allocation. We secured one on Kilmacormick Avenue through the intervention of Senator P J O'Hare, who was on good terms with the Unionist Mayor, Richard Barton.

Our move into the private housing sector came through a timely tip off. A Welsh firm with a base in Enniskillen, Slack and Parr, had a beautiful Georgian house on Willoughby Place, just 15 minutes from the school. It had been occupied by their foreign sales manager who had recently been asked to leave his position. The new incumbent's wife was unwilling to move to Northern Ireland during the Troubles, so he opted to spend the weeks in a local hotel, flying home every weekend and releasing the property for sale. Knowing all the local auctioneers were either Masons or diehard nationalists, the company opted to sell privately. I visited the factory to make my bid, was subsequently told I had a counter bidder, and to make my way to the company's offices at 3pm on a designated day to resolve the matter. When I arrived, I found my bidding rival had brought with him an auctioneer, a man whom I knew would be determined not to let a Catholic buy property in such a prestigious, predominantly Protestant area. Fate was on my side when the Slack and Parr manager pointed out to my rival that he would be paying £200 of his bid straight to the auctioneer and so would need to bid an extra £400 to match me. He then asked the auctioneer to leave, which he did, with a bad grace. My rival then upped his bid by £15. I raised mine by £250 and the house was mine – more bluntly, my rival told me to "stick it!" The manager then contacted the factory's solicitor, Noreen Cooper, to instruct her to pass on the papers to my solicitor. When told who the house had been sold to, this bastion of Unionism challenged him "do you know what you are doing?"

"Yes, I think I do," the manager replied, calmly.

"It is not advisable to sell your house to that man," she insisted, knowing full well I was listening.

He stood firm and instructed her to hand over the papers. She put the phone down on him. "Now you know why I was selling this house myself," he told me wryly.

Our family, by now seven in number, delighted in moving to this beautiful, spacious 17 room house that was three stories on one side, four on the other. These houses had been built in Georgian times when the army rewarded distinguished military service with a plot to build on. At the time we bought the house the area was predominantly Protestant but in our years there many other Catholic families moved in nearby and it became quite mixed.

And what of the relationship with my mother? In time, there was some "meeting of the waters." She was a loving and loved Granny. Patricia, however, felt there were always little notes of criticism and she never felt fully accepted as an O'Connor. Perhaps that is stereotypical of mother and daughter-in-law relationships; perhaps it was my mother's abiding belief that no one was good enough for her only son. My mother always remained very kind to me, making sure I didn't need to buy a suit, a shirt or a pair of shoes.

By now, my sister Kathleen had long since made her own life in Omagh. She had married Hugh Ward, the principal of Beragh school, and worked as a midwife. I am glad to know the younger generations of Wards and O'Connors keep in touch; I see their banter on social media sites.

Scouting, at least for Catholics, didn't exist during my childhood. It was very much the provenance of the Protestant community, like the Boys' Brigade and Church Lads' Brigade. I remember when I was about 14 seeing a Jamboree of English Scouts in the Square at Forthill and being mightily impressed by what I witnessed. The neatly pressed uniforms, the discipline, the activities, the performances – there was so much to admire. My interest was reawakened by the arrival in Enniskillen from Castleblayney in 1962 of a dynamic and most persuasive young priest, Fr John

McKenna. Fr McKenna had been involved in the Scouting movement in Monaghan and was on a mission to bring it to Fermanagh. First, though, he set about organising activities for young married couples and asked myself and the deputy manager of the Bank of Ireland, Brian McNerney, to help. These comprised talks on family affairs, finances, and medical matters, all designed to be supportive to young couples starting their life together. His next mission was to recruit us as founders of Scouting. For perhaps seven weeks in succession we travelled to Castleblayney to meet Paddy Downey and see his troops in operation. We were impressed and convinced. First, we needed premises. My old first school at Abbey Street was lying derelict. Fr McKenna was possessed of a rare charisma and never knowingly failed in his powers of persuasion. While the Erne hospital was being built on one side of the town, so our first Scout Hall was coming to life in another. Builders and tradesmen of all genres and traditions gave willingly of their time, materials and services. Some from the Protestant community had their own involvement with and respect for the Baden Powell or "English" Scouts and were keen to see many of those benefits extended to the Catholic community. The renovated premises had two floors – upstairs for the Guides and downstairs for the Scouts, though, at that time, never the twain did meet.

Brian and I were appointed the first leaders and we began by recruiting eight boys from local schools. Eight girls were also recruited for the Guides, so our development ran parallel. This group of eight patrol leaders then trained another eight who had been recruited as deputies. Progress was rapid. Within two to three years we had a couple of hundred Scouts and Guides. In 10 years, that had doubled to 400, with 42 leaders. The town had been waiting for a constructive and positive outlet for its young, and supported us so well. Enniskillen quite simply took Scouting to its heart, where it has remained. At our parades to Mass, on St Patrick's Day and Corpus Christi, we were always accompanied by a band. These were proud and splendid occasions, but they got me thinking, why not our own band? At this time, state or Protestant primary schools had a ready supply of musical instruments for pupils to learn to play. Not so CCMS/ Catholic schools, which had to raise 20% of their own funds, rather than have everything supplied by the Department of Education. I began a civil rights campaign to have parity of opportunity and in time the Western Education and Library Board agreed to supply musical instruments to two Catholic primary schools, The Convent and St Michael's Boys. As these young musicians moved on to second level education, so too did the provision of instruments, while the Board provided the primary schools with more for the next generation of pupils. It was a remarkable breakthrough, and all because of our campaign. And, of course, we had our own band who played for the first time at a parade in 1976. We thought they were fantastic! Though in retrospect and in the light of the heights they would one day achieve, I must concede that they were perhaps not that tuneful after all....

Our growing Scouting numbers had forced a move in premises to the old St Michael's Primary School – where insurance was to become an issue – and then later to the gym at the present day St Michael's, but a subsequent change in the Education Board's practices prompted a rethink. Under the new terms, we would have had to pay for the use of the gym and the services of a caretaker, costing us as much as £5,000 a year. The solution was obvious: we would build our own Scout Hall. The local GAA club had just invested heavily in buying land for a pitch and clubhouse and finances were strained. They were delighted to sell us a quarter of an acre for £4,000. Our finance committee of eight then began fundraising in earnest by visiting 10 businesses in the town per week to ask for a donation of a £1000 each. That first night, we raised £7,000: an impressive start. The campaign extended to include funders, trusts, every conceivable source of income. The Bank of Ireland was approached about a loan and agreed on the condition our committee would hand over the deeds to their homes as security. This was too high risk and unfair on some members so instead we approached the AIB where Seamus O'Connell happily advanced us £50,000! We ran draws, the public rallied behind us and thanks to an excellent team of volunteer workers led by the outstanding Brendan Conway

(RIP) and the dynamic Tommy Quinn, the Hall was built and kitted out within 11 months, opening on 4th December 1994. By now, I had been instrumental in setting up Scout troops across the county and this was a wonderful focal and meeting point for them all. As part of the Diocese of Clogher, we had links to Scouts in Donegal, Louth and Monaghan and it was a great shame that during this time leaders and parents alike were reluctant to travel north to meet us. Meetings always involved us travelling south, often to Clones, with the inevitable harassment from UDR patrols shown to what was clearly a car full of nationalists on their way to and from the Republic. This was one of the

Each of these companies and organisations donated over £1,000 to the building of the Scout Centre

more invidious signs of the times and blatantly sectarian. That said, the local police did get involved in drill training with our Scouts and we established positive relations and cooperation with the Baden Powell Scouts in the area. Our Hall was the envy of them all!

The Scout Band gradually grew in numbers and the standard of their performances improved greatly. With the financial help of the Ulster Arts Council, we acquired new instruments and we also availed from the extra tuition our members received from Bob Quick and Stephen Magee, tutors with the Western Education and Library Board Music Service. The Fermanagh County Board GAA and then the Ulster Council looked for the band to play at the County Championship games every Sunday. This gave the band a very high profile. When the Ulster Final was moved from Clones to Croke Park, between Armagh and Donegal, we got our first opportunity to play there. As a result of our performance that Sunday we were invited back several times to Croke Park to play at All-Ireland Football and Hurling Semi-finals in front of crowds of 70,000 and with it a lot of national and international television coverage.

The band played at many sporting, concert and festival venues throughout Ireland, England and Scotland but the highlight of our experiences abroad were our trips across the Atlantic to New York and Boston. On these trips - thanks to the help of the New York Commissioner for Scouting, Gary Schiller, Larry Morrish of the US Military,

Mary Nolan, US Irish Emigration, and Richard Kennedy and Marshal Sloane, Century Banks, Boston - we were hosted by The Coast Guards on Governor's Island, The US Army at Fort Hamilton NY, Boston College and Regent College, Boston. Fiona Smith, Nollaig Cleary and Coast Guard John St Lawrence did Trojan work in arranging our programme of activities in the US. The band performed at several concert venues throughout the two cities but the highlights were playing in front of packed venues such as The Mets Stadium, NY, and Fenway Park in Boston for the Red Socks.

Many of our former members have followed a career in music. One in particular comes to mind. This young lad started playing at eight years of age. His parents returned the instrument because they could not afford the £10 insurance fee. Because he performed so well in his aptitude test, the principal, Bro Peter, paid the fee. That eight-year-old became the lead cornet player with the London Philharmonic Orchestra.

I would later have the honour of being appointed Scouting District Commissioner. In this role, I helped in the development of Scouting throughout Fermanagh. I later became Commissioner for Northern Ireland and became elected to the National Executive Board of The Catholic Boy Scouts of Ireland. I also was instrumental in acquiring the purchase of Castle Saunderson with the help of Martin Shannon which is now a major cross border international

Scouting centre on the Fermanagh, Cavan and Monaghan border. I spent two years in the US fundraising for the wonderful project. I am proud that the movement I co-founded in Enniskillen nearly 60 years ago, remains thriving to this day.

Leading St Michael's Scout Band at Croke Park, 2009

St Michael's Scout Band at the annual Ulster football final in Clones

Two years of age with my sister, Kathleen

Kathleen and me on our Confirmation day

Kathleen and me with our father, Phil

With the P6 Class, Brother Adrian and Brother Louis, 1952 – I am third from the left, front row

2

CIVIL RIGHTS

Many of the injustices I had campaigned against all my life were brought into focus by the publication in 1968 of *Fermanagh Facts*. Compiled by Frank McManus and Colm Gillespie, this publication highlighted the gerrymandering, anti-Catholic discrimination and injustices prevalent in the county, with very specific and damning statistical evidence. In a council area with a 60% Nationalist majority, Nationalists held only 40% of council seats, due to shameless gerrymandering of electoral wards and the ghetto system. A nationalist electoral area with 1,800 voters might elect only one councillor, while a Unionist area with 6-800 on the electoral role could return many more. Employment discrimination was rampant. 80% of local government posts were held by Unionists. The new Erne hospital had 14 ward sisters, only one of whom, the night sister, was a Catholic. Of the Western Education and Library Board's 72 bus drivers, just two were Catholics, and only one of the 12 ambulance drivers based at the

Erne hospital. The figures spoke for themselves. All job applications required the applicant to state their religion. Every teaching appointment, whether in a state or Catholic school, demanded that the new incumbent swear an Oath of Allegiance to Queen Elizabeth. I recall when I went to swear my oath before taking up my post at St Michael's, the JP, a Unionist, said to me, "I'm sure you don't want to read this," and duly signed it for me without a word being uttered. It was virtually impossible for Catholics to buy property in the town of Enniskillen, as all the auctioneers were Masons. I had first-hand experience of this myself when purchasing Willoughby Place. Only in the licensed trade did Nationalists dominate, due to the influence of the Temperance Movement in the Protestant community: there were only two Protestant owned pubs in the town!

Consequently, there were few opportunities for ambitious young people in the Nationalist community. Of the 56 boys pictured in my school photograph in Chapter 1, only six would remain in Enniskillen. The choice was stark: educate or emigrate. There was no work at home. For myself, the choice was to educate. The 11 Plus revolutionised opportunities for young Nationalists, offering bright youngsters the opportunity of second and third level education based on ability rather than birth-right or financial standing. We were the first wave of this and proud to be so. The majority of my classmates at St Michael's College went on to become teachers themselves and contribute greatly towards enhancing the new opportunities on offer. One classmate, Peter Quinn, was unusual in that he opted to go to Queen's University, Belfast, to study accountancy. This was a major breakthrough for a Catholic student from Fermanagh. Frank McManus, co-author of *Fermanagh Facts*, also broke the mould by training first as a teacher and then entering law. Otherwise, the only entry into the legal profession for a young Catholic was if there was a practice already in the family to return to. Medicine and Veterinary careers were, almost without exception, the same.

The civil rights movement was officially launched in 1968 and I was immediately to become a committee member. We held meetings in parish halls, and organised major street rallies. The mood of the Nationalist community was steadfastly behind us. We had no difficulty in attracting 10,000 – 12,000 people to a street demonstration. They came from all age groups and walks of life and our numbers included some members of the Protestant community who were opposed to the blatant discrimination evidenced in everyday life. One stalwart of the committee who merits mention was Bill Barbour, a teacher at Portora Royal. We were invariably met with hostility and obstruction from the police, who would put up barriers and warn us that we were holding an illegal assembly. We in turn would sit down to try to block the road – though space was always cleared for the bastion of Unionism, Noreen Cooper, to drive through in her car with its customised number plate of 1690!

One Saturday afternoon, in the summer of 1969, we planned carefully to divide into five or six separate groups and block all the major roads leading into Enniskillen. I was among the group at the Cornagrade Road when the police moved in and arrested 38 of us. They carefully targeted those they perceived to be the ringleaders, arrested us, and took us to the town's police station where we were held in the gym. Fortuitously for the police, the town's Resident Magistrate, McCrea Elliott, clearly forewarned of the police's intention, was available for a special court sitting on the Saturday afternoon. We were marched in custody to attend the hearing, passed a group of police officers who kicked the legs from under us. There was no mention of legal representation. We were jointly charged with obstructing the police in the course of duty and remanded in custody to Crumlin Road jail. We were held in solitary confinement in B wing. We were permitted half an hour's exercise in the prison yard, twice a day, provided we walked in silence and remained two metres apart. We quickly established a method of communication through the prison toilets, leaving scribbled notes on toilet paper for the next visitor! I remember listening to a broadcast of the Ulster Football final between Cavan and Down in my cell on the Sunday. I could hear the broadcast from a patient's radio sitting on the window ledge of the Mater Hospital next door to the Crumlin Road prison: a match I had planned to attend! On the Tuesday we were taken through the tunnel to Crumlin Road courthouse where all but three of us were released on bail. Remaining in custody with me were Eamon Cox, an accounts manager and prominent civil rights activist like myself, and a young fella from Dublin who had been up for the day, liked the spirit of the protest and joined in! We never even knew his name or anything about him but, as he came from outside the jurisdiction, the unfortunate lad could not get bail – quite an introduction to the civil rights movement. We were remanded in custody to appear at Enniskillen Court the following Tuesday.

By now, we had received written communication from a priest and the NICRA, the civil rights association, which ensured its Belfast members brought us in silver service meals – we were treated like lords. We were also gifted hundreds of cigarettes. As a non-smoker, I used to pass them down on the prongs of the fork to the boys in the cells below. I was instantly very popular. The NICRA also ensured that a civil rights solicitor from Belfast would represent us in Enniskillen. The court appearance was theatrically dramatic as this young teacher and Scout leader, with an unblemished record, was led into the dock in handcuffs. The judge gave us a stern dressing down for our behaviour. I responded by telling the court he was a very sectarian judge but that I wouldn't have expected anything else, adding that, one day, I expected to be sitting in his place and would do better. My remarks, made in open court, were duly recorded.

We were each fined £8. I refused to pay, but a benefactor paid it for me. My mother and my sister Petronella were in court throughout. Afterwards, my mother remarked, "I hope that's enough of that carry on," but I sensed with her political leanings she was quietly proud of me. My wife Patricia was also supportive and committed to the civil rights campaign. My mother's situation was slightly uncomfortable in that she now lived next door to Marcus Lyle of the Special Branch, a man and his wife who were very good to her.

Undeterred, my activism continued. We occupied houses that had been unfairly allocated, perhaps to a single, childless Unionist applicant over a Catholic family with several children. The council's powers over housing had been removed and given to the newly established Housing Executive. Indeed, the council's powers had been reduced to the alliterative "bogs, bins and burials."

NICRA protests were carefully coordinated so that action in Enniskillen could take the focus off events in Derry, Armagh or Belfast and ensure the police response was more dissipated. The NICRA was a broad church with clear divisions; I found many of the older, more conservative members were committed in spirit but lacked the will or energy for active street protests or confrontation. Perhaps partly because of this, I had, since its formation in 1968, been active in the student led People's Democracy movement. I was just two years out of student life myself, and empathised with its more radical ideology. This was reinforced by the brutality of the attack by the security forces and Loyalist protestors on their peaceful Belfast to Derry march at Burntollet Bridge – one of the seismic events in focussing world attention, for the first time, on the appalling discrimination and brutality of life in the north.

With the birth of the SDLP under the leadership of Gerry Fitt in Belfast and John Hume in Derry, the NICRA waned. Sinn Fein was also gathering momentum as a political party, although its members retained their abstentionist stance. I felt it was a pity that a movement that had enjoyed such massive popular support, uniting people in a common idealism and cause regardless of age, status, background and in some cases religious affiliation, was now being divided. A friend and neighbour named Jim Donnelly, a newly elected SDLP councillor, asked me to stand for the party. I declined. I later turned down a similar approach from Sinn Fein. It wasn't for me.

However, throughout the 1970s I remained active in many campaigns, highlighting and protesting against the injustices of internment, taking part in the rent and rates strike, supporting the Blanket protest, demonstrating against conditions in the H Blocks and supporting the hunger strikes.

Much of my focus in the years leading up to 1977 was on my beloved Scouting. Never had there been such a need for focussed, constructive, positive activity for teenagers. It kept countless youths out of trouble, away from paramilitary involvement and street violence, during the darkest days of the Conflict. As part of the national Scout Training Team I ensured all our leaders were properly trained for their role. I was elevated to International Team Training in London. The role played by Scouting in everything from peace-keeping to improving the quality and aspirations of young, impressionable lives in the 1970s can never be underestimated.

With the teaching staff of St Michael's Primary School, 1980 – I am third from right, back row

One of the many school teams that won the Fermanagh Primary Hurling League, trained by me

Teaching in St Michael's Primary School 1970

Patricia and Bernard with their first child, Philip, 1966

On a civil rights march in Enniskillen, 1969 – I am furthest on the right

3

THE ARREST

I was awakened from my sleep in the early hours of the morning by continuous banging on the front door of my house and the persistent ringing of the doorbell. It was Thursday 20th January 1977 at approximately half past five in the morning. The door was being thumped with fists and boots and the knocker kept being loudly banged and the bell continued to ding. I jumped from my bed shouting to my wife who was still asleep that something was wrong. I ran to the middle front window of our bedroom which overlooked the front door. To my amazement, there below was a large number of policemen, policewomen and army personnel. The dazzle and shine of the streetlights opposite our house on the peaked caps of the police made them stand out among all the soldiers. The street was lined with army Land Rovers and there must have been between 15 to 20 police and soldiers. On hearing the banging on the front door, the first thought that struck me was that there was something wrong. I thought they were calling to give us bad news about my Aunt Christina, who was due to undergo a serious operation in Cavan Hospital that day. On seeing the huge squad on the steps to my front door and along the footpath below I quickly changed my mind. I said to my wife, who was more asleep than awake, "For God's sake, get up quickly, we're going to be raided or something."

I quickly ran down the stairs in my pyjamas, and hurriedly opened the glass panelled middle door. Sticking through the letterbox of the front door and pointing at me was the barrel of a rifle. The black front door of our house opened inwardly in two halves. The soldier had to take the gun out of the letterbox to allow me to open the right-hand side of the front door. An English accent, presumably that of one of the soldiers said, "Come on, come on, don't be so long about opening the f****** door!"

As I opened the door, two soldiers came charging past me saying that they were going to search the house under the Special Powers Act, or words to that effect. I was speechless. I just remember thinking to myself, "Good luck to you searching this house for anything!"

More soldiers, I don't know how many, continued to pour past me into the hall. They were followed by two policemen, one of whom held a large sheet of white paper in his hand. He stood in front of me and placing his left hand on my shoulder asked in a very formal manner,

"Are you Bernard O'Connor?"

"I am," I replied, wondering what all this was about.

I had not to wait very long for this information. The policeman proceeded to read from the sheet while his companion stood to the left, looking on.

"You, Bernard O'Connor, of 38 Willoughby Place, Enniskillen, are being arrested under section 12 of the Emergency Provisions Act, for having knowledge of explosions, armed robberies, having explosives and arms in your possessions ..."

He continued to read on and by this stage I could feel myself beginning to laugh with shock in reaction to the whole thing. When he had finished reading, I looked at him in disbelief and said to him in a bold inquisitive way, "You must be joking." He quickly assured me he was not.

I still stood in the front hall in a shocked, speechless state. The smaller of the two policemen, with a black moustache sticking out from under his nose, asked if I would like to put some clothes on. I said that I would and I proceeded to go back up the stairs to my bedroom. When I got to the top of the stairs, I encountered my wife, Pat, who had been having a discussion with two soldiers and a policewoman on the landing outside our bedroom door. Pat turned to me and said that one of the soldiers had ordered her to have all our seven children, the eldest of whom was 10 and the youngest, Nollaig, aged 10 days, wakened and brought downstairs to the front room. I turned to the soldier I took to be in charge and asked him not to disturb the children at that hour of the morning because they would get frightened and might panic. I pointed out to him the bedrooms where the children were sleeping and told him to take a quiet look into them but not to search them until the children got up for school. He seemed quite pleasant and agreed to my request. The two policemen escorted me to my bedroom and watched me dress. I could hear soldiers going everywhere throughout the house especially the attic bedroom and the storeroom above my bedroom. I put on my brown suit, cream shirt, brown and yellow tie and brown round necked jumper. I was feeling quite cold and shivery so I also put on the top of my brown tracksuit. I said to the policemen that I was feeling cold but one of them assured me that I would not be cold in the car. When I was dressed, I sat down on the bed and I put on my socks and heavy brown shoes. All the time I was thinking of my poor wife and seven children. Pat was only a few days home from hospital after having a baby. She was confined to bed because she had to have an operation at the birth. I had been doing all the household work at home for the children for the previous two weeks. I was feeling very worried.

Having now fully dressed, one of the policemen asked me did I want to wash or go to the bathroom. I was escorted by the two police to the bathroom where I washed and had a shave with my electric razor and brushed my teeth. The two custodians of the law escorted me down the stairs to the hallway below. This was one of the saddest parts of the whole operation. While being brought down the stairway with a policeman on each side of me, I looked up and there at the top of the staircase looking down at me was my 10-year-old, auburn haired son, Philip, with a pale frightened look on his face. I could have cried.

I said to him, "I'll be back tomorrow."

He did not answer.

The second saddest part of my arrest was meeting my wife at the hall table and saying to her that I was being arrested. She began to get annoyed and asked the policeman, "What are you arresting Barney for? Sure, he did nothing." The policeman did not answer.

I took all the stuff out of my pockets, such as driving license, letters, keys and money and left them on the hall table. I could feel the two policemen holding me by both arms and gently heading for the front door. I could hear my wife crying to the police not to take me away until the army and all were gone. As I was being pushed out the front door, I shouted back to my wife that I would not be long away. I was held tightly by my arms and brought to a police car sitting about 20 yards down the street from my house. The small policeman got into the back seat of the brown Cortina and I was pushed in next, followed by the tall policeman. A third policeman was sitting in the driver's seat with the engine running and on the passenger seat sat a large black gun which I saw from the inside light of the car. The taller policeman told the driver to move off. He then produced a pair of handcuffs from his tunic pocket and told me to hold out my hands.

I said, "There is no need for them."

He replied, "I am acting under orders."

I held out my hands and he proceeded to handcuff them together, one across the other; when fastening them he adjusted them as tightly as possible. I felt really insulted and humiliated. I was being treated as a criminal. I could not understand the point of this handcuffing exercise. Surely, if handcuffs were not needed to take me from the house to the car, what was the point of putting them on in the car, wedged in the back seat between two police officers and a third in the front with a large machine gun at his side? The morning was still dark and the road was wet where it obviously had rained during the night.

ARREST UNDER SECTION 12 OF THE PREVENTION OF
TERRORISM (TEMPORARY PROVISIONS) ACT, 1976.   56/77

1. Name of person to be arrested *Bernard O'Connor*

2. Address *38 Willoughby Place*

3. I arrest you under Section 12 of the Prevention of Terrorism (Temporary
    Provisions) Act 1976 as I reasonably suspect you of being concerned/having
    been concerned/in the commission, preparation or instigation of acts of
    terrorism.

4. Date of Arrest *20/1/76*

5. Time of Arrest *6. AM.*

_____   _____
Station of arresting member   Signature and Rank of
                                         Arresting Member.

My arrest order at 5.30am on Thursday 20th January 1977. Take note of the date – 1976.
It was a year out of date!

4

TRIP TO CASTLEREAGH

One of the policemen told me in the bedroom that there was not much need for extra clothing as the heater would be on in the car and in fact, he was telling the truth. The engine of the car had been kept running as had the fan heater and the parking lights. The driver of the car did not look at me or say anything to me. He just responded like a robot to the orders from his colleague, "Right, drive away."

The car had to drive past my home in order to get to a large turning area in the road at the entrance to Portora Royal School. That school has been famous down the years for producing outstanding people such as Oscar Wilde. Harry West, then leader of the Unionist Party, was a member of the school's Board of Governors. As the car turned and sped past my home on its way back into town, I looked to my right and saw all the five front room windows fully lit and at least three army vehicles parked along the footpath in front of the house. I felt the muscles of my stomach tightening and a very sick, frightened feeling coming over me. I was worried about what might be happening inside my house. Would the soldiers be tearing up floorboards or destroying the wallpapered walls which I had spent many hours decorating for days and nights? More importantly, I was worried about Pat and the seven children, especially the new-born baby.

I was also extremely upset and puzzled by the logic of this entire operation. Here I was in the back of a police car after being accused of a large number of serious crimes and then arrested. I remember thinking to myself that when I get to the Enniskillen Police Station someone will explain. I believed that the inspector and or the police detective, who had been a good neighbour to my mother since my father died, would be able to clear up this unbelievable situation and let normality prevail by bringing me back home.

On reaching Enniskillen RUC Station, which was about half a mile from my home, I discovered that neither of these men could help me for I was not taken out of the car. Instead, after entering the main gate, the car was driven over to the left of the main station entrance and parked in the drill area. It was here that I used to watch the police recruits drilling every morning for the first 15 years of my life when I lived in the public house at the bottom of Queen Street.

One of the policemen got out of the back of the car, leaving more room for myself and his colleague. The other two policemen began smoking and having a conversation about cars and the Motor Show in Belfast. It was still very dark outside but during my time sitting in the backseat I could see a number of police cars coming into the courtyard at irregular intervals. Within a period of about 30 minutes at least five other cars arrived. I could see that a number of people were inside but only one policeman got out of each car and went into the police station, where the policeman that had been sitting next to me had also gone. I was getting the impression that a number of others like myself had also been arrested but I had no idea who they were as I could not see due to it being so dark. It seemed like a full hour passed before anything happened.

While waiting there I remember thinking about a previous time when I had been arrested and wondering if this was going to be a similar affair. About three years previously I had been returning home on a night from playing bowls in St Michael's Community Centre when I was arrested in a rather dramatic fashion. On my way home from the Community Centre, I was accompanied by Eamonn McIntyre, a fellow bowler, and to whom I was giving a lift home as he also lived on Kilmacormick Avenue. We had no knowledge of it, but seemingly an explosion had taken place in a building along the road that we took. I wondered why so many people were standing out at their front doors in the housing estate as we drove in. I asked my wife who was standing at our front door what was wrong, and she replied that a bomb had gone off somewhere. At that very moment, as Eamonn was getting out of my car, another car came charging into the street and parked right up at the front bumper of my car. A man jumped out and ran up to me on the footpath, caught me by the arm and twisted it up behind my back with his other hand. I heard a click of something metal and felt something hard pressing into the back of my left ear.

A voice said to me, "O'Connor, your game is up."

I recognised the voice to be of the inspector I knew at the local police station. Eamonn McIntyre tried to reason with him.

"That man has done nothing wrong. He has been playing bowls all night," Eamonn told him.

The inspector paid no heed to him and as my wife came running from our front door towards him, he pointed the gun which had been at the side of my head at her and shouted in a loud voice to all the neighbours who had gathered around, "Anybody moves in this street and he's dead!"

I was questioned for two days and kept in Enniskillen Police Station until all my routines were checked out. All the questioning was straightforward and there were no threats or abuse. There was no way I was involved in the explosion that night as I had been playing bowls with about 30 people from 7-11.30 pm.

I thought that this situation would be more of the same. Of course, I was aware that anyone who was deeply involved in civil rights and the People's Democracy, as I was, was always classed as a prime suspect even of terrorist activities. It is always good propaganda for the authorities to try to smear those who fight for civil rights with acts of violence.

My thoughts that this arrest was going to be something like the previous arrest got a severe setback when the policeman finally came back to the car. He got into the backseat again and his words were, "We're soon ready for the road." I couldn't believe my ears. I asked him where they were taking me. He replied, "Belfast, Castlereagh if you've ever heard of the place."

It was all getting like a bad dream and each bit of it was getting worse by the minute. I had heard of Castlereagh before from items in the newspaper describing the tough methods of interrogations used there, but I always treated such newspaper articles as propaganda. I would dismiss them, feeling that those in Castlereagh were probably all terrorists anyway, and were exaggerating the treatment there for their own ends. I had been influenced by the old saying "No smoke without fire," which resulted in my not having any real fear of going to Castlereagh, as I thought I had nothing to be worried about.

Between half past six and seven o'clock our car moved off. My theory that other people like myself were arrested that morning took a step nearer the truth when at least four other cars moved off at the same time. We were about the fourth car in the line moving out through the barracks gate.

From what I could see there were no army vehicles present. I don't think it fully struck me that we were on our way to Castlereagh until that moment. The only other time I experienced feelings like these before was when my father died in the Royal Victoria Hospital in Belfast on the 22nd of May 1965. I had a deep feeling of sadness coupled with despair. Even the dark damp streets of Enniskillen that morning seemed lonely and empty. No traffic, no people, not a sight nor sign of life at that unearthly time of the morning. The only time I ever before experienced the streets of Enniskillen on a winter's morning was going to first Mass at six o'clock on a Christmas day. However, the only similarity was the time of the morning, all the other factors were as different as day and night.

The three police constables spoke freely to each other on the way to Belfast. The main subject of conversation was motor cars. This was basically because the driver of the car had been to the Motor Show in the King's Hall, Belfast the previous day and he was keen to relate to us his new-found wealth of knowledge of the latest in the automobile world. The conversation was carried on in three levels which became apparent as the journey went on. The driver of the car and the policeman on my left were regular members of the RUC while the policeman on my right was a member of the police reserve. I knew him to see in Enniskillen. This became obvious from the trend of conversation. Questions and comments were made freely between the two regular policemen while their reserve friend's contributions to the conversation were treated often with a silent response or a changing of the subject by one of the regulars. Several times during the journey I experienced a similar reaction. I, being a qualified driving instructor with the Department of the Environment for Northern Ireland, felt I could contribute to any conversation about cars and their performances as I had a vast experience of cars during driving lessons and tests. I had a school of motoring with my brother-in-law, Hugh Ward, and gave lessons at weekends and after school every evening in Enniskillen. However, I felt my contributions to conversations in the car were unwelcome to say the least. The only policeman that showed an interest in anything I said was the reserve guy. In fact, he even gave Polo mints to me. It was a bit awkward having to use both hands to hold a Polo mint and put it up to my mouth owing to the handcuffs. The only time I succeeded in getting a positive involvement in a conversation during that terrible journey to Belfast was when they were talking about the performances of the different police cars in the cortège. We were on the stretch of motorway between Dungannon and Belfast at this stage. The convoy of cars began passing one another out. Our driver would make comments about the performances of the other police cars. I asked him how long the police kept their cars before changing them.

"About a year," he replied.

I asked him what they did with the old cars.

"Sell them," was his reply.

I asked him how much they would be worth. The policeman on my left then told me that the police cars were sold at a special sale in Belfast for roughly £600 each. He went on to say that they were always in really bad shape after a year of hard driving where they received a lot of abuse. He said that the engines were generally run out of them but that the body work was generally in fairly good nick. The consensus of agreement between them was that they would be good value even if the engine had to be replaced.

The level of conversation lagged back to long periods of silence and I had a long period of thinking time again. The conversation helped to distract me from the terrible situation I had ahead of me and what I left behind at home in Enniskillen. I felt that the only help I could call on at this stage was from God. I always had great faith in the Rosary, so I was able, with the help of the fingers on my hands, to say the Rosary twice during those long periods of silences. The only Mysteries that could come readily to my now confused mind were the Sorrowful Mysteries.

For the last 10 miles or so of the journey, it had gradually turned to daylight but the sky was cloudy and dull. On reaching the outskirts of Belfast the convoy turned off the motorway at Stockman's Lane, but took a turning which brought me through a part of Belfast which was unfamiliar. I had been a student in Belfast for three years and had got to know the city reasonably well, but this route was not known to me. I could now see the other cars in front, but I could not recognise anyone in them. Finally, with much changing of roads and meandering through the small streets of Belfast, we turned right into an entrance to a large wired-off car park in front of a red brick building. We were let through the barrier at the entrance and followed a silver metallic Cortina around the back of the building. The car in front pulled up at the side of the wall opposite the back of the building. I saw a youngish fellow being taken from the car and being brought in through a black door. I did not recognise this young man at the time but later knew him to be Owen Curry from Derrin Park, Enniskillen. I was then taken from our car by my two police escorts and the one to the left of me in the car took me in through the same black door as the other man. Once through the door, he took a key from his pocket and unlocked my handcuffs. What a bit of relief that was. The tightness of the handcuffs had made my wrists sore and the tops of my fingers go numb, particularly the little fingers of each hand.

The following is my wife's account of the arrest.

On Thursday the 20th January 1977, I was awakened by loud banging and the doorbell ringing. It was approximately 5.30am. As I sat up in bed my husband was at the middle window of our bedroom looking out.

I yelled something like, "My God, what's wrong?"

At first, he answered, "I don't know." Then he said, "Christ, we're being raided."

I kept thinking, "My God, what's wrong? What can have happened? Why should we be raided?"

I had often heard of homes being raided, but those things only happened elsewhere and to other people. I got out of bed as quickly as I could; I was just a few days out of hospital after giving birth to my seventh child by caesarean section. As I had had six normal deliveries I was still not over the shock or the effects of having had an emergency operation. As I left the bedroom, having pulled on a dressing gown and slippers, I met two soldiers on the landing. One of them asked me to get all my seven children into one room. As I knew how terrifying it would be for the children to be woken from their sleep by men with guns, I protested. At that point my husband came back up the stairs escorted by two policemen. I told him what the soldier had requested. My husband spoke with the soldiers and I went downstairs to the front hall where I saw another policeman and a policewoman with about four other soldiers. It was a very frightening experience but as I did not know at this point that my husband was being arrested, I asked why they had come at such an unearthly hour and what did they want? I told them that I was just out of hospital and not well enough for such an upset. The army officer in charge said that they were going to search the house. I kept shouting, "What for? And why, at such an early hour?"

I then lifted the telephone receiver, opened the telephone book and dialled a number. I was told by the policewoman that I was not allowed to use the phone. I answered, "It is my home and my phone and I will use it if I like." There was no reply from the number I had dialled so I pressed the button to get the line back.

"Who are you phoning?" the policewoman asked.

"My MP," I replied.

I was then told that I could not use the phone and it was taken from my hand.

By mistake I had dialled the phone number of Frank Maguire's public house in Lisnaskea instead of his home. I still kept asking the people in the hallway, "What is this all for?"

Just then my husband came down the stairs with two policemen. I looked up at the three of them and asked again,

"My God, what is this all about?"

Barney answered me, "I don't know, Pat, I only know that they're taking me." I will never forget the feeling I had at that moment because up until then I had no idea that he was being arrested. I started to shake.

Barney emptied all his belongings out of his pockets on the hall table beside me. He then put his arms around me and said not to worry, he would be home soon. When I realised that they were not all leaving I said that I was not going to be left with all the armed soldiers and police on my own and that they were to leave my husband in the house until they were all going. Someone said, "You will be all right Mrs O'Connor, the policewoman is staying."

I can assure you that at that moment his words were of no consolation to me. My eldest son was standing at the turn of the staircase and I told him to go back to bed. I then told one of the soldiers that I wanted someone to go with them on the search and was told that no one could enter or leave the house until they were gone, that I must accompany him before and after the search to ensure that they did no damage to anything, but that I must remain in the downstairs drawing room during the search. The soldier who appeared to be in charge of the others who were going to do the search took a notebook and Biro pen from his jacket and I had to go with him to each room in my home: 17 rooms in all and five flights of stairs. By the time we got to the basement I was hardly fit to walk. I told him that there was an enclosed yard and garage and two dogs in the yard. He told me that they had a dog with them too, round in the entry at the rear of our home. I have never been able to understand why our dogs didn't bark; they may have been barking when the commotion was going on at the front door but as there was so much noise I couldn't have heard them. They never once barked during the next three or four hours.

We returned to the front room. I was told to bring any valuables in the house to the drawing room. I said that my husband had a coin collection upstairs and the policewoman escorted me to the bedroom to get it. She carried the albums of coins to the drawing room and the search commenced. About five soldiers did the actual search with one acting in charge of them.

In the drawing room were a policeman, a policewoman, an army officer and myself. The army officer appeared to be in charge and was addressed as "Sir" by the RUC personnel. He was very pleasant and well-spoken and knew a lot about the history of Portora Royal School which is almost opposite our home. The policeman and he were very interested in Barney's coin collection and spent a considerable time looking at it.

About half an hour after the search started the soldier in charge came into the drawing room and handed me about £70 which had been on the dressing table in my bedroom. Sometime later a soldier came into the room and handed the policeman what appeared to be a small sheet of notepaper. I heard him say that it appeared to be a speech. I went over to the sofa where the policeman was sitting and told him that it was the words of a song which I had copied from a record many years previously. The song was, 'Take it down from the mast, Irish traitors.' The policeman put it into a bag. A short time later he suggested that it might be better to get dressed as it was getting chilly and the policewoman escorted me to the bedroom and stayed until I was dressed. My infant daughter was still asleep in her cot and I remember saying a silent prayer that she would remain sleeping until this ordeal was over.

Another scrap of paper was given to the policeman by one of the searchers. It contained the words of another song, written by a Fermanagh man and entitled, 'Only our rivers run free'. I remember saying to the three in the room that I felt that I was having a bad dream, and for what reason could this be happening? I remarked that Harold Wilson had said that we were all entitled to our own political beliefs and that I believed that there could only be peace in Ireland when it was united. I said that I was entitled to my opinions just as they were entitled to theirs and the officer in charge agreed. At approximately 8.00 a.m. Philip, my older son, came to the door of the room and asked if they should get dressed for school. I said "Yes" and about 15 minutes later he returned with Nuala, Maire, Sinead and Brian and asked if they could have their breakfast. The five children had their breakfast in the dining room and then returned to the drawing room.

During the search of the record cabinet great interest was shown in a record entitled The Price of Justice. This is a record of Republican songs and the proceeds of the records went to the dependents of the prisoners in Long Kesh. On the sleeve were the photographs of two men who were allegedly beaten up by the British Army. I was asked by the officer, "Is that what you think of the British Army?" I replied, "I don't think about your army at all." I then told him that he would also find a record featuring King William on a white horse if he would like that also and that he would find all kinds of music in our house. No one was interested in the Orange record. An empty cassette tape was also given to the police. I remarked that it was a blank tape and offered the use of the recorder to try it, but the offer was refused.

At approximately 8.30 a.m. the soldier in charge of the search asked me to accompany him back around the house to ensure that no damage had been done. I went with him to the attic, the bedroom and living room, but was unable to go any further and said that everything seemed to be in order and that I would take his word that the basement and outside were the same. I thanked him for having broken nothing and for not terrifying my children any more than their presence had done. He thanked me and said that they all had a job to do and they liked to do it as agreeably as possible.

We returned to the drawing room. The searchers left and I asked the Commanding Officer and the policeman if I would get to see my husband later in the day, or would he be home? The policewoman, having conferred with the policeman, told me that Barney was in Castlereagh in Belfast and was being held under Section 12. I asked what that meant and she said that he could be held for seven days. As she was going past the hall table she wrote down a telephone number on an envelope that was lying there and told me if I phoned that number and asked for the Detention Centre I could enquire about my husband.

They left my home at 8.45 a.m.

5

CASTLEREAGH DAY 1

The area inside the small black door, which was enclosed on two sides and covered over with galvanized iron, consisted of a small yard running down between the two temporary-looking grey hut structures. Looking down the yard, the building to the left was of red brick and one storey while the hut to the right of the yard was a one storey wooden structure which I found out later to be used for medical examinations, fingerprinting, filing of records and meetings between members of the Special Branch and CID. Both of these buildings ran the full length of the yard which was at least 100 feet long. The entrance to the red brick building to the left was roughly about half way down the side leading from the yard. The entrance to the wooden building was in the gable of the rear end. Opposite the entrance to this building was a small shelter used as toilets. The surface of the yard was covered with small chippings with grass growing through. At the end of this yard, facing me, was a wall of between 30 to 40 feet high while behind me was a two-storey grey-black building with two sets of iron steps leading up to the two doors, one for each storey. There were about five iron steps leading up to the door to the ground floor; steps which I was to trudge up and down for many times during my stay in Castlereagh.

The first place I was brought to that morning was inside the wooden building on the right. I was taken into a small office by the uniformed policeman I had been handed over to after being brought through the small black door. Sitting behind the desk in the office was a uniformed sergeant of the RUC. He said he wanted a few particulars from me. He asked me my name, age, date of birth, height, religion, address, name of wife and each of my children. Everything was carefully written down. The only amusing thing was that when I came to the names of my seven children I had to spell them for him. All my children, except for the eldest, have Irish names. He is called Philip Joseph after my late father and his deceased brother. The RUC are mainly a non-Catholic force whose members would obviously have difficulty in spelling Irish names.

I was then asked to hand over all my possessions. I searched my pockets remembering that I had emptied them before I left home that morning. However, in the back pocket of my trousers I found an English £1 note. There was nothing else in any of my pockets. I put £1 note on the desk.

"What about your watch and ring?" he asked.

I took them off and put them on the desk.

"Search him now," the sergeant told a tall policeman who was standing in the open doorway of the office. I stood up and the policeman searched me thoroughly. The only thing he found was a silver chain around my neck with a Miraculous medal on it. This too I had to part with. Then I was told to take off my shoes. "Give me your laces," the sergeant asked. I began to think that I was going to have to walk around in my sock soles but this fear was soon discounted when I was told to put my lace-less shoes back on. My belongings which now consisted of one wristwatch, one wedding ring, £1 note, one medal and chain and one pair of laces were put in a large brown envelope and my name was written across the front of it. I was then taken from the office and brought out of the wooden building into the yard and then up the five iron steps to the door to the cell block. The policeman knocked on the door a few times. A bolt was pulled back on the inside and the door opened. I stepped inside with the policeman. Inside this building was a long wide corridor with grey doors to the right and left. There was a table and two chairs inside the main door. I again had to give my name and address to the uniformed policeman behind the table. All was written down in the large book. I was then taken to one of the grey doors about halfway down the corridor. It had 'G8' on the door. The door was opened with a key and I went inside. The door was locked behind me.

The cell was better than I had expected. It was a small

room about four metres long, three metres wide and three metres high. An iron bed with a hair mattress stood opposite the wooden door. Sitting folded on top of the mattress was a pair of white starched linen sheets, two white pillow cases and two white woollen blankets, spotlessly clean. In the corner of the room was a grey plastic chair with a red padded seat. The cell had hardboard walls and the ceiling was sheeted with plasterboard. The floor covering was a grey vinyl type. Heating pipes ran down along the wall beside the bed and near the floor and were always very hot. There was a ventilation grille on the wall above the bed which I was just able to reach when standing on the bed. No light came in through this grille which was covered with a thick, heavy metal cover with a diagonal criss-cross pattern. There was no natural light getting into the cell, instead it was lit by a circular light which was about a foot in diameter and screwed to the wall opposite the bed. I had no way of putting this light on or off. The door was on the same wall as the light fitting. In the centre of the door was a small, magnified eye hole which gave the police a full view of the prisoner in his cell. I put my coat over the back of the chair and sat down on the bed. It was the first time since the events of that morning that I was able to have a good hard look at myself and start to do some solid thinking. I was in an unbelievable situation and asked myself some very real questions: "Why me? What's ahead? How do I get out of this mess?"

I would later learn from bitter experience the importance of having a full medical examination – I was wrong to refuse one at this point.

I had not too long to analyse the situation when the following routine happened, which became a horrifying experience for me during the coming days.

Knock! Knock! Someone got up from a chair, went to the door of the cell block. A bolt flew back. A voice said, "O'Connor." The heavy footsteps led down the corridor to my door and stopped. A key was turned in the door. It opened. "Come along," a voice said, "O'Connor." Two uniformed members of the RUC stood there as I came out. "You have to see a doctor," one of them said.

I was taken out of the cell block, down the five iron steps and brought out of the wooden building to the left of the yard, which I had been in earlier. I was brought into a room marked 'medical room'. Sitting at a table in the medical room was an oldish grey-haired man with gold rimmed glasses which he looked over at times to talk to me. He asked me my name and address etc., which he wrote down on an official form. When he heard that I lived on Willoughby Place, Enniskillen he said that that was the most beautiful part of Enniskillen. I asked him if he knew Enniskillen well. He went on to tell me of how he had enjoyed a most wonderful holiday there a few years previously and that he had stayed in a guest house on Willoughby Place. He then asked me if I knew Mr and Mrs ----------- of Willoughby Place as it was in their guest house that he had stayed during his holiday. I had often played bowls with ------------- but, he being a staunch Unionist, and I being an active member of the civil rights movement, we never conversed much with each other to say the least. Of course, I did not express my thoughts to the doctor.

I was then asked by the doctor if I wanted a full medical examination. I replied that I did not. This I was to find out was a huge mistake. I went on to explain to the doctor that apart from suffering from a rather heavy chest cold I felt otherwise all right. The doctor then asked, "Have you been taking anything for the chest cold?" "Mysteclin capsules," I answered. He then explained that he did not have any Mysteclin there, but that he would prescribe Penbritin. He counted 24 of these capsules into a small brown bottle, wrote my name and the instructions on the front. He said I would receive two capsules four times a day and that the supply should last three days. If I needed any more he would give them to me. He told me that the policeman on duty would give me the capsules at the proper time. He then asked about my job and family. I told him that I was a schoolteacher and that I was the father of seven children.

When I left the medical room, I was escorted back to my cell by the uniformed policeman who had remained waiting for me outside the door of the medical room. The doctor gave this policeman the capsules to bring back to the cell block with him.

Again, I was brought up the steel steps, the door was knocked, bolt drawn, door opened from the inside and in I went. On my way up the corridor I had met two civilians, one with a large camera and case hanging from his shoulder while the other plain-clothed man had a small blackboard and a folder. One of them asked the policeman who was bringing me into my cell who I was. On being told "O'Connor" he checked his list and discovered that he had to photograph me. The two cameramen accompanied me into my cell. The one with the ginger beard began loading up his camera and getting his lens focused while the other put the blackboard down on the bed and began writing on it with chalk. I was told to stand at one end of the cell. The blackboard with my personal details written on it was given to me and I was ordered to hold this in front of me while the other man took two or three photographs. They then packed up and left without saying anything to me. The cell door was then closed and locked once more. The attitude of both the plain-clothed men made me feel a little edgy. They were very unfriendly and had ordered me about like a criminal. I anxiously awaited my next call.

I had not too long to wait before the ritual began again. The now familiar knock on the cell block door. The bolt going across. The name O'Connor being mentioned. Footsteps sounding on the long walk to my cell door, then the key being inserted, the lock opening and the same words, "O'Connor, come on."

I sat on the side of the bed on which I had been lying, slid my feet into my shoes and headed out the door. There I saw a tall, slim, sharp-nosed but pleasant man from my home town. He signed the large book on the table along the corridor and then he brought me out of the cell block and into the wooden building. I was led into a room on the right of the corridor just beyond the medical room. He was quite friendly and asked me how I was getting on. I told him that I was all right. When we reached the small room, there waiting for us was another Enniskillen CID man and another detective whom I did not know. He was a sturdy, rough featured man with a very cunning look on his face. He went into a small room off the one which we were in. I was told to sit down.

Lying on the table was the sheet of paper which a policeman had read to me while I was being arrested that morning. I tried to turn it round so that I could read it and also see whose signature was at the bottom. However, it was lifted by one of the detectives who began reading it himself. I asked him to read it out to me as I had got such a shock that morning that I was unable to remember what it said. He did so. I then asked him who had signed it but he declined to tell me this. I was then told to go into the next room. In it were bottles of chemicals, and sheets of paper were lying on a high desk below the window. I was asked to proffer my right hand and the detective began to paint it with black ink. I now knew that I was being fingerprinted.

Both hands underwent this process, first each finger, the combination of fingers and finally different positions of my hands. These were all done in duplicate. I was fascinated by the whole process because I had never seen it done before. When the detective had finished, he poured a yellow spirit over my hands and cleaned off the ink with paper tissues. He threw the soiled paper into the bin, which at this stage was full. None of the detectives conversed with me during the entire process. I was then brought back to the cell block. I was not worried by the fingerprinting operation because I knew that there was no way my finger prints could be matched up with any act of terrorism.

I lay down on the bed once more and began thinking of what might happen next. I knew that it could not be long until I would be interrogated. I could feel my heart giving an extra beat every time I heard the knock on the cell block door and the bolt going back. I waited for the name O'Connor to be mentioned. When it wasn't I felt relieved. I began praying for help. I started the Rosary. Again, the only Mysteries I could bring to mind were the Sorrowful.

First – The Agony in the Garden.
Second – The Scourging in the Garden.
Third – The Crowning with Thorns.
Fourth – The Carrying of the Cross to Mount Calvary.
Fifth – The Crucifixion and Death of Our Lord on the Cross.

It was difficult to concentrate on each decade. Firstly, I had no Rosary beads and secondly my mind was jumping from one thing to another – home, wife, children, school, Enniskillen, Castlereagh, what's next, etc. I had just enough time to say a Rosary which took about eight to 10 minutes, when the routine started again. Knock, bolt across door opens, mumbled talk, step after step down the corridor, stop at my cell door, key in lock, rattle of turning keys and finally my door opened. The moment which I had been dreading had arrived.

Bernard O'Connor   D.O.B. 21/6/42

ss 38 Willoughby Place, Enniskillen   OCCUPATION:: _Arbitrator_

informed on being taken into police custody at __9.05__ a.m./p.m. on

__/77__ at Castlereagh Police Office that I had been arrested by a constable

Section 12 of the Prevention of Terrorism (Temporary Provisions) Act 1976 on

~~able~~ suspicion of ~~being concerned~~/having been concerned/in the commission,

~~ration~~ or instigation of acts of terrorism.

informed that any request or complaint about my treatment when in custody should

~~de~~ to an Inspector of the R.U.C. or to any other policeman as soon as possible.

~~ITS (If any)__ Yes __

ollowing is a complete list of my property which was taken from me by the

Tch.	added 3.45 pm 22/1/77
~~...~~	Newspaper (Fermanagh News)
~~...~~	2. Novels (Ashit, August & SEAN)
~~...~~	Glasses & Deathtool
~~...~~	4 Pairs shoe
	1 1st Victory V 3gungun
	20 lug

ture X B O'Connor.   Date 20/1/77   Time 9.05 ~

DEPARTURE

~~...~~ O'Connor   ADDRESS 38 WILLOUGHBY PLACE
       Enniskillen

~~...~~ that during the time I was held "in arrest" at Castlereagh Police Office, I

~~...~~ treated and had no injuries inflicted on me by anyone.

~~have no complaints to make~~

wish to make the following complaint _Complaint made to Dets._

~~...~~ certify that all the property listed above was returned to me (~~with the~~

~~...~~)*

ture B O'Connor.   Date 24/1/77   Time 9.15 am

~~late as appropriate.~~

My Castlereagh arrival form

Medical Examination (Initial/Intermediate/Final) at........ _Castlereagh_ 56/77

Police Station on (date)....20.1.77........(time)........ _10.05_

Name....Bernard O'Connor........ Address.... 38, Willoughby Place,
.... Enniskillen

Date of Birth....2/6/62.

I,....Bernard O'Connor........ wish/do not wish to be medically examined.

I am/am not alleging assault or ill-treatment.

Signed....B O Connor........ Witness.... _[signature]_

Requests treatment for chest cold. Has cough with
greenish sputum. Has previously had :-
R. Penicillin 250 mgm.
2 x 4 times a day for 3 days .

To have Ferilone tablets if he gets indigestion

I agree/do not agree to whatever medical treatment may be thought desirable.

Signed....B C Connor........ Signature of Examining MO.... _[signature]_

Witness.... _[signature]_ .... Date....20.1.77........ Time.... _10.45_

Status.......

My first medical examination with a police doctor - Dr Page

6

FIRST INTERVIEW

"O'Connor, you are wanted for interview," said the uniformed policeman standing in the doorway of my cell. I slipped my feet into my lace-less shoes and followed him down the wide cell block corridor. There, standing at the table, writing on a large sheet of paper, was a tall plain-clothes policeman. When he had finished writing, the door of the cell block was opened and I followed him down the steel steps. This time I was not brought into the wooden hut where I had been previously but instead, I was taken to the brick building running parallel to it. The door to this building was halfway along the side facing the wooden building. The detective who was escorting me carried a cream-coloured folder under his arm and kept the hand of that arm in his pocket. I followed him into the interrogation block, as it would be called by subsequent detectives. A dark, narrow corridor ran up the centre of this building with blue painted doors opening into small rooms to the left and to the right of it. I was led into one of the doors on the right, later known to be room four. Standing in the middle of the room was another well-dressed plain-clothes detective. The room itself was about 12 feet long and nine feet wide. At one end of the room was a table and three tubular framed chairs. Two of the chairs were on one side of the table and the other chair was on the opposite side. There were two windows in the room, both with small panes of frosted glass, which were covered by an iron grille. The floor of the room was covered with a dark brown underfelt material while three of the internal walls were covered with a pegboard tile material, about a metre square. The fourth outer wall was made of brick and was coated with a dull and shabby cream paint, clearly applied many years previous.

As I entered the room behind the tall detective the other smaller detective moved against the wall, keeping his hands behind his back. He did not speak. The big fellow threw the cream-coloured file on the table and, pulling me by the arm, ordered me to stand at the other side of it. He lifted the folder up again, flicked through a number of pages, and then threw it down on the table again. I saw that my name was written on the front of the folder.

"So, you're Bernard O'Connor," said the big fellow, looking sideways at me with a half smirk on his face. He paused a minute while he looked me up and down. Then he commented, "Man, but you're an insignificant little bastard."

Words spoken in hate which I shall never forget for the rest of my life.

All the while his companion stood against the wall and did not speak. I felt rather frightened and apprehensive of what was to follow after such a blunt introductory comment. I was then invited by the tall blonde detective to tell him something about myself. I was speechless for I was again confused, and I did not know where to start in telling him who I was or what I did, I just stood there looking at them both.

"Are you f****** deaf or something?" demanded my interrogator.

I said, "No."

"Well then, start f****** talking," he shouted. Again, the attitude was very aggressive and the language was tough and rough. I told him that I was 34 years of age, a schoolteacher, and that I lived at 38 Willoughby Place, Enniskillen with my wife and seven children.

Suddenly he came storming across the room shouting, "When you're f****** talking to us you'll not f****** stand like that!"

He ordered me to get up on my toes and to bend my knees keeping my heels off the ground. He pressed down on my shoulders with his hands so as to make my knees bend enough. When he had me as low as he wanted, he then told me to hold my arms out straight in front of me and to stay like that. All these instructions were frequently elaborated with the word "f******."

"Good God," I thought, "What is this man trying to do to me?"

He then walked round behind me and slid his toes under my heels so as to make sure that they were off the ground. I was told not to dare to move from that position. Several times I felt like over-balancing. My legs were shaking. I was again ordered to start talking about myself, particularly as regards politics and civil rights. I said that I was a member of the Fermanagh Civil Rights Committee and also a member of Fermanagh People's Democracy. The big fellow demanded to know how I could be a member of both "outfits." I told him that basically there was very little difference between the two organisations. The main reason for the formation of Fermanagh People's Democracy was that the Fermanagh Civil Rights Committee was more inclined to talk about injustices and highlight them in the media while the People's Democracy in Fermanagh was more interested in highlighting these injustices by actions such as squatting, street demonstrations and civil disobedience. The People's Democracy in Fermanagh was mainly a pressure group forcing the Fermanagh Civil Rights Association to take action.

Having given this explanation, I subconsciously relaxed. The tall detective walked around behind me and discovered that my heels had touched the ground and my arms had begun to sag. I received a sharp slap on the ear from behind me and was commanded to, "Get up on your f****** toes."

My arms were then pushed roughly back up into the desired position. I was beginning to feel the strain of remaining in this awkward stance for so long. The other CID man had remained in the same spot and still did not speak. Frequently he would lift the folder from the table, glance through it and then put it down again.

My interrogator was very interested in my civil rights involvement. He questioned me thoroughly about the many acts of civil disobedience in which I had been involved during the years 1968 to 1972. He would frequently walk in front of me and punch me in the stomach or slap my face and ears with his open hand when I allowed my knees to bend or my arms to sag. He asked me if I ever slapped the children at school. I told him that I had slapped children on occasion for serious breach of discipline or for acts of vandalism. He then informed me that like the children I too would have to be disciplined and learn to do as I was told. My punishment was earned by not standing in the required position.

Obviously, it was important to them to make me feel afraid and to give me the impression that they, the police, were in the position of authority where I must do as I was told. They seemed to be sizing me up by watching my reaction to them. The hard/soft tactic was being used on me, with the big fellow playing the "tough" role and the smaller acting more "softly."

Having fully and thoroughly discussed my involvement

with the People's Democracy and the Civil Rights Association and my reasons for being actively involved, I was then asked which political party I belonged to. I told them that I was not a member, nor did I wish to be a member, of any political party. The tall detective told me that it was impossible for anyone who was so committed to the active side of the civil rights movement as I was, and especially as I was a member of a revolutionary group like the People's Democracy, to have withdrawn from public political life completely at the end of the civil rights campaign in 1972. He went on to say that the civil rights movement was a front for the IRA. Therefore, as I did not go to political meetings in 1972, I must have gone underground and become a member of the IRA. I protested at this accusation, stating that I never was nor did I wish to be a member of the IRA or any other paramilitary organisation.

That was the comment which really set the tall detective mad. He came right over to me and punched me heavily in the stomach. I staggered back against the wall which was about two or three feet behind me.

"Get back on your f****** toes" he shouted.

Bending down over me and looking right into my face he told me that he didn't know anything about me until he read bits of my file a few minutes before meeting me. He went on, "You f****** Provos all come here and come out with the same stuff. You're not members of the IRA. You don't believe in violence but before you're very long in here you're all singing like birds, even those of you who are trained to resist interrogation."

He lifted the folder off the table and began reading extracts from it to himself; he continued to make such comments as, "My God. Good Christ. You bastard" etc.

He put the folder back on the table, looked at me and said, "For a school teacher you are a right bastard. Not only are you up to your neck in the IRA but you're the f****** godfather of the Fermanagh Unit. By the time you get out of here you'll have every charge in the book thrown at you."

I told him that he was obviously talking to the wrong person. There must be someone else in Enniskillen who should be in there instead of me. I did not have any connections with the IRA nor with their political group Sinn Fein.

At this stage the other detective spoke. He advised me to come clean and confess for my own good. He explained to me that innocent people are not lifted from their homes in the early hours of the morning and brought to Castlereagh for fun. He advised me to make things easier for myself by making a statement telling them everything I knew. I again protested my innocence, but it was to no avail. The attitude of the man who was now speaking was friendly in comparison to the other. I was by now perspiring freely, my legs were trembling, for I was having great difficulty in keeping my heels off the ground, especially with no laces in my shoes, and my arms felt like lead. The detective obviously saw my plight and he asked if I would like a drink of water. Of course, I told him that I would, and he left the room and returned shortly with three white plastic beakers filled with water. He put them down on the table saying, "Now Bernard, there is no truth drug in these so you can have your pick." I lifted a beaker and drank about half the water in it. The two detectives also took one each. I was then asked if I had had enough to drink. The friendlier of the two detectives then wrote the letter "B" on my beaker and placed it in the window ledge to keep it from being spilled. I felt slightly better after my drink, for not only had the water refreshed me, I had also taken the chance to stand up straight while drinking it.

I was again cross-examined for at least another hour about my involvement with the civil rights movement and the People's Democracy. Once again, I had to resume the by now familiar squatting position. I continued to deny any involvement in terrorist activities despite numerous punches and slaps in the face. It had got to the stage where I accepted that I was going to get hit often. The only thing that was puzzling me was how I could convince them that I was innocent.

The interview lasted between two to three hours. At the end of the session, I was told by the tall man that he was now putting me back in my cell, but that I would be like the rest of the Provos and write a confession within the next few hours. He was the one who brought me back to the cell block and signed me in again. Throughout the interview the smaller of the two men neither threatened nor abused me in any way.

7

INTERROGATION 2

I lay down in the bed and gave several sighs of relief at being away from my interrogators. I was more confused than ever. I had just been through a couple of hours of sheer mental and physical hell. What were they trying to get me to confess to? I was accused of being the "godfather" of the Provos, a terrorist, one unfit to be a teacher and a parent, yet they did not accuse me of any particular incident. What sort of stuff were they reading about me from the folder which was about half an inch thick with foolscap typed pages?

I knew that I had not taken part in violence. I now also knew that these men were out to prove the opposite. I lay quizzing myself up and down as to what I would do. I again resorted to prayer. I said a Rosary in thanksgiving for reacting so coolly and placidly to the tall, cruel Branch man. I felt that so often one prays to God for help that it would be a good idea to pray to him in thanksgiving and what better person to thank God for me than Our Lady, His blessed Mother. Throughout the Rosary I could find my mind wandering back to the previous interview. It was particularly hard to concentrate and keep count of the various decades. I again used the Sorrowful Mysteries as I felt they were more appropriate.

I hadn't long finished the Rosary when the footsteps came down the corridor and stopped at my door. It opened. I thought I was for it again. Into my cell stepped a uniformed policeman with my dinner on a plastic plate with a white plastic knife and fork. The dinner consisted of a meat pie, beans and potatoes. I was also given a plastic beaker of tea and two small red paper-covered Tate and Lyle packets of sugar cubes. The food was left on my chair. The door was locked again. My stomach at this stage felt full and the sight of food made me feel sick. I tried to eat a few of the beans but I found myself starting to retch. I could not get myself to eat. I tried a second time to try and eat and wash it down with a drink of tea but again I could not face it. I drank most of the tea into which I put two of the sugar cubes. The other packet I put into my pocket. I intended to eat them later as sweets.

I lay down on the bed again and began to think over the whole of the last interview. Once more I resorted to prayer, for I felt that the only person that could help in the present situation was God. I said a full Rosary asking him for help to withstand another interview like the last one. I had now been in my cell for at least an hour when the heart stopping ritual began again. Several times I heard the cell block door opening with the door bolt going across and then mumbled conversations followed by footsteps down the corridor. Each time my heart was in my mouth. Would they stop at my door? Inevitably, my turn eventually came. On reaching the table in the corridor I met another plain-clothes CID man. He ushered me out of the door and led me to the interrogation block. We went down the corridor and went into room five, which was about half way down on the left. The number was on the outside of the door.

This room was similar to the previous one: felt-covered floor, three peg-board walls, with one brick wall on the outer side. In the room were three men. I stood in front of the table and quickly glanced at each of these plain-clothes detectives. I was told to take a seat by a fair-haired middle-aged man wearing a maroon blazer. I did so. On the other side of the table sat two other detectives; the third pulled his chair round to the side of the table beside me. These men were friendly and each introduced himself in turn. The man who sat beside me was stout and well-built and smoked a crooked pipe. The man directly opposite me at the table wore a wine-coloured blazer and had fair hair. The third wore a light blue suit and had curly fair hair. The interview was begun by the oldest detective. He said, "Well. Bernard, I suppose you know by now what you are in here for." He looked very surprised when I told him that I did not. He then remarked that I had not been "a very good boy" in Enniskillen for a number of years. I asked him what he meant. He continued to talk to me between puffs of smoke which he was attempting to suck from his pipe whilst making numerous efforts to light it. He accused me of being actively involved in the Provisional IRA in Enniskillen. He said that I had brought explosives from Swanlinbar to Enniskillen and that I had taken part in car bombings which had wrecked Enniskillen in 1972, as well as other explosions in the same year. I emphatically denied that I had any connections with Provisional IRA, never mind taken part in their activities. I suggested that he was talking to the wrong man. At this all three began to get involved in the discussion. The man in the wine blazer did a lot of writing. He noted details of my address, my family and my employment. The first detective, the eldest one, suggested that it must be very hard for a school teacher to support a family of seven children financially, never mind purchase an elaborate dwelling on Willoughby Place. He suggested that I had bought my house with the proceeds of an armed robbery at McDermott's Supermarket in Enniskillen. I laughed at the idea but soon had to change my attitude when he opened the folder and read an extract from a page. This referred to a fictitious person who was only mentioned as "I." This person stated that he had been instructed by Bernard O'Connor to keep a watch on McDermott's Supermarket for several nights, and that he had also kept watch on a certain night while two others took a box of money from McDermott's van at closing time. The money had then been given to this unnamed "I" before being handed over to Bernard O'Connor. Hence, I had obtained the money to buy my house.

The detective set about proving this mathematically on a piece of paper. He asked how much my home had cost. He told me that at the time of the purchase of my home my bank balance was below £500. I agreed and felt surprised at them knowing of my personal financial dealings in the bank. He then asked me where I found the money to buy my home. I told him that I was a member of the National Association of Schoolmasters and Teachers Union (NAS) and that I had applied through them to the Colonial Mutual for a 100% house loan. In the meantime, my bank manager granted me a bridging loan to buy the house pending the Colonial Mutual loan being available. Therefore, I was able to purchase my house. He then tried to figure out how I was able to keep such a house, a large family and drive a large car and manage financially. I was amazed at the information he had about my financial situation. He was able to account for my income right from my salary, family allowance, and school of motoring fees, and on the other hand mortgage repayment and cost of keeping the house going. When the totals were all added up and balanced out the subject of the armed robbery was no longer discussed.

The next matter for discussion was my relatives. I was asked to give details of where my mother and sister lived. They enquired about my aunts and uncles living south of the border. Of course, these questions were asked in such a way as to let me know that they already had the information. For example, I was asked what relatives I had in Arva, Co. Cavan, and who was related to me in Dublin. They told me that my relations in Scotshouse, Clones were decent people. I was then asked for details of where my wife's family were from and their close relations living in Belfast.

The same kind of phraseology was used in the questioning so as to let me know that although they were asking these questions, they knew the answers full well. However, they did seem surprised when I told them that a first cousin of my wife, Jackie Bohill from Downpatrick, was a detective in the RUC and visited us while a recruit in Enniskillen Police Station.

Having recorded all the details of my finances and my relations, the topic switched to myself. I was told that even at nine years of age I had been "a bad boy." I again asked the detective to elaborate and he duly obliged. He reminded me of an incident back in the summer of 1951 when more than 20 nine and 10 year olds like myself went to explore the old unused sawmill belonging to Achesons at the water's edge along the Brook. We discovered a box of old steeples which we used to fire, with the aid of elastic bands held between the fingers and thumb of our hands, catapult style, at the water hens flying across the river. Someone had reported this prank to the police and it was now being used by my interrogators as evidence of my misdemeanours.

I was then reminded of my days in the civil rights

movement between 1968 and 1972. Extracts were quoted in great detail from civil rights speeches which I had made during the campaign. Details of my arrests for taking part in a sit-down protest and a banned civil rights march in Enniskillen were read out to me. All aspects of my involvement with Fermanagh People's Democracy and the Civil Rights Association were related to me and everything they told me was exactly correct.

The details of my family were once again investigated in detail. The full Christian names, date of birth, schools attended and the activities of my children were all discussed thoroughly. My responsibility towards my children was emphasised to me and I was told that it was of prime concern to my interrogators to get me back to them as soon as possible. On numerous occasions I was reminded that my wife would be unable to cope with seven children alone, especially as she had undergone a caesarean operation for the birth of our last baby just a few weeks previously. It was repeated that their whole concern was to get me back to my wife and children. Of course, for such a release I would have to tell them all that I knew about terrorist activity in Enniskillen. I said that I had never been involved in any such activity in Enniskillen. At this the third detective quickly interrupted and pointed out that by saying that I was not involved in any activity meant that I may be denying any actual acts of terrorism but that I was really admitting that I had been involved in the setting up and the planning of these activities, having lacked the courage to do them myself. From that point on I would emphasise my denial of involvement in terrorist activities by saying, "I have not been by thought, word, or deed involved in terrorist activities."

At this stage of the interview the third detective rose from his chair, pulled a small slip of paper from his pocket and held it in the palm of his right hand. He walked round to where I was sitting, held the paper in front of my eyes and told me to read it. Written on the paper was the name, "Constable Purvis." I was asked if I knew Constable Purvis. I said that I knew a Constable Purvis of the Police Traffic Branch who visited schools to give road safety talks to the children. "Not him, stupid," was the stern reply. The detective went on to tell me that I knew damn well that the Constable Purvis on the note was the constable murdered in Enniskillen by gunfire from a passing car. I told him that I recollected such an incident happening some years ago but that I had not known the name of the man who had been shot. I was then told that I knew everything about it and that before I left Castlereagh, I would be charged with the murder of Constable Purvis.

The other two detectives said that they had no idea what their comrade was talking about but they felt that I was definitely involved in illegal activities, otherwise I would not be in Castlereagh. They went even further to point out that as the information about me during the civil rights campaign and the facts of my personal life had been so accurate, therefore the information about my involvement in terrorist activities must also be correct. They explained that it is easy to get involved in terrorist activities without being fully aware. They went on to tell me that I had been involved from the beginning by helping to ferry injured men to hospital across the border in my car.

"Surely you are not ashamed to say that you acted in a Christian way by helping injured men?" the first one said. "I would do that myself," he continued. I denied any such involvement. The same accusation was repeated during interrogations in the days to come.

Each of the detectives in turn kept urging me to make a confession to some trivial offence which had happened in Enniskillen. All the offences they referred to had happened four or five years previously. They read from the typewritten pages in the cream folder and then accused me of being involved in yet another terrorist offence. I kept denying any involvement whatsoever and told them that they had the wrong man. Again, they encouraged me to make a confession in a friendly and fatherly way so that a deal could be done for everyone to save face. It did not matter how trivial the offence. They would get off the hook for having arrested me and I, in return, could possibly secure my release.

The first detective was particularly persuasive. He sat close to me on my side of the table and at times put an encouraging hand on my shoulder. He pointed out that in the event of having a fringe involvement with the IRA it would result at the worst in me having to appear in court, and they would see that the court would be lenient to me. I again emphatically denied any involvement with the IRA. It was pointed out to me that I was being given a great chance to get out of a tight situation, but if it was found out later that I was lying I would not get the same opportunity again. In such an event, even murder charges could be proffered against me. I again stressed to them that they were talking to the wrong man.

About halfway through this interview the third man left the room and did not return. Several times during this interview the door would open and one or sometimes two men would look in and make a comment like:

"That's him. That's O'Connor, he was there."

I did not know any of these men at that time but I met them at subsequent interviews.

At the end on this interrogation session, which seemed to last three to four hours, I was brought back to my cell block by the second fair-haired man. On leaving the room, the man that did most of the talking told me that of all the men in Castlereagh he could help me most and if at any time I felt that I had anything to tell him, I was just to ask for him and he would be available straight away. I thanked him for his help and for being so kind and considerate to me.

8

INTERROGATION 3

It was now after six o'clock on that Thursday evening and I was back in my cell. I lay down on the bed for a few minutes and tried to figure out the whole situation I was in. I was feeling very thirsty and my throat was extremely dry. I knocked on the wooden door of my cell and immediately a policeman came and asked what I wanted. I told him I wished to go to the toilet. He opened the door and brought me to the toilets which were further along the corridor on the same side as my cell. I urinated in the toilet and when I came out I asked the constable for a beaker to get a drink of water. He put me back in the cell and told me that he would bring me a drink, which he did. The water was ice cold and very refreshing.

I lay down on the bed again and began saying my Rosary of thanksgiving. I couldn't keep a count of the Hail Marys or concentrate on the Mysteries which were still the Sorrowful ones. In fact, I couldn't think of the other Mysteries of the Rosary to use. I was using my fingers to keep me right in counting out the 10 Hail Marys for each decade of the Rosary but even with doing that I still lost count and often said an extra five Hail Marys to make sure I had said a full decade.

My tea came and it consisted of a fried egg, beans and chips. I did not feel like eating but I decided that I should force myself to eat as much as I could so as to give me strength to be able to cope with the mental strain I was being put under. I had to eat slowly so as to avoid vomiting the whole lot out again, and if not for washing it down with tea, I would never have been able to finish it. The feeling was one of trying to eat a dinner after having a four-course meal. The paper plates and plastic cutlery did not make the meal any more appealing, never mind the other factors. After tea I again resorted to prayer. I said another Rosary in preparation for the next interrogation so that with the help of Our Lady and the good Lord Himself I would be able to withstand any pressure imposed on me. Despite similar difficulties as before, lack of concentration and bad counting, I managed to get through it before I was again called for interview.

I was signed out of my cell block and brought back to the interview room by one of the three detectives who, along with two others, had interviewed me during the afternoon. One of them was also there waiting to interview me but he left after about an hour and a half, leaving me on my own with his colleague. I was asked if I had thought over the idea of making a statement since my last interrogation. I said that I had nothing to make a statement about. I was then told that I was being very foolish in not co-operating. Sooner or later, I would open up or confess, so why not start now and get it over and done with? I said that I would not confess to anything which I had not done. I said that there was one of three things wrong: the first one was I being framed by someone; the second was someone had, under interrogation at some time or another, given my name knowing of my innocence in order to get themselves out of a tight situation; and third was the police had made a terrible mistake. He assured me that the police had not made a mistake, I had not been framed and that I was definitely the man they wanted. I tried to convince them over and over again that I never had any act or part in violence at any time in my life, but they would not accept this.

After the first detective left, his comrade told me that I should accept his advice, for if there was anyone in Castlereagh who was sincere and genuine it was him. He said that I should accept the deal which I had been offered earlier that afternoon. I would be a terrible fool if I didn't, he pointed out. I was being let off the hook, according to him, by being asked to sign for a trivial offence but he threatened that some detectives would later be putting more serious charges against me for which I could get life in prison. I pleaded with him to see my side of the story, but to no avail. I stressed to him that I was not involved in any crime so why go on pressing me to sign statements to the effect that I had done something that I did not do? Several times during the interview my interrogator raised his voice in anger at the fact that I was still not willing to accept the help of those who were genuinely interested in me. He shouted at me that he believed I was a member of the IRA and that I was leading young boys astray.

During this interview I had cause to become very frightened, not of my interrogators but of the noises and sounds which I could hear from other rooms in the interrogation block. From the room immediately next to the room I was in I could hear detectives screaming and shouting at the man they were interrogating. The inner walls of the interrogation centre were a wooden framed cavity structure with acoustic peg board tiles attached. Several times the walls would shake with the thud of someone being thrown up against them. On at least three occasions I was told to not pass any remarks on what was going on in the next room and assured that such treatment was not for me. From what I could make out from the shouting, someone was being accused of being in possession of a gun. The language being used was very crude and very abusive. Several times I could hear loud screams of pain and pleas: "Please don't! No! No! No more! No more! No more!" For a time, everything would go quiet and then the whole turmoil would burst out again, worse than before. At one stage a detective could be clearly heard to shout: "You've destroyed my shirt with your f****** Fenian blood!"

Despite the assurance that I would not be subjected to this kind of treatment I was still terrified. This was not the only room from which those kinds of sounds were coming. In at least two other rooms similar activities were being carried out. In the room opposite to the one I was in, on the other side of the corridor, a person was constantly banged against the door and the walls. The sound echoed down the corridor. I could not make out what was being said in this room. In another room further down the corridor similar sounds could be heard, but more faint. I was so frightened and concerned about what was going on in the other rooms that at times I wasn't listening to my interrogator. He told me that he would never resort to that type of behaviour. He said that he always found that if he was honest with others, others were honest with him. The interview ended with me being back in my cell before 10pm. I knew the time because I had a look at the interviewer's watch shortly before the interview ended.

9

INTERROGATION 4

Being back in my cell was a great relief to me. Despite assurances that I was not to be given the same treatment as what I had just heard, I was not fully convinced and as a result I felt very apprehensive. However, now that I was back in my cell, away from it all, I thought I would be there for the rest of the night as it was now around 10pm. I had just finished another by now confused Rosary when the bolt went back on the cell block door and someone entered. I heard the name O'Connor being mentioned in the middle of a jumbled conversation. The dreaded footsteps came down the corridor and stopped at my door. My hope that I was finished for the night came to a sudden ending when I was told that I was wanted for interview again.

I was brought by a uniformed policeman to the table at the end of the corridor where there was a plain-clothes CID officer bending down over the table signing the relevant form for my release for interrogation. Having done so he ushered me in front of him through the cell block door, down

the now famous steel steps, across the narrow yard and into
the interrogation block. There in room five stood another
CID officer. He was about six feet tall and I recognised him
immediately. He was once a uniformed policeman in my
hometown of Enniskillen. The detective that had escorted
me to the room was a good looking, well-groomed man
while his companion was coarse and rather tough looking. I
was told to stand at the back of the room. The rough looking
man, who held the now familiar cream folder in his hand,
said that up until now I had refused to cooperate and make
a statement. He said that I was obviously guilty and that
unless I was ready to write confessions his patience would
not hold out for much longer. I told him that I was innocent
and had nothing to confess. He told me that they were there
to prove the opposite. By this time, he had left the folder
on the table and was standing right beside me. I was asked
what way did I want it from now on? I looked at them and
enquired what was meant by that. Without replying the
tougher of the two men drew his arm out and landed me a
punch in the jaw. I fell back into the corner and ended up
lying on the floor. In my fall the lace-less shoes came off my
feet. This man then lifted one of the shoes and fired it at me,
just missing my head, and it banged against the wall beside
me. I was told to stand up again in the middle of the floor
and the other detective told me that I now knew what they
meant. At this stage the man who had hit me was reading
from the file and he then commenced to ask me the same

questions which had been put to me at the previous three interviews. I kept denying all the allegations about me being involved in terrorist activities and continued to impress my innocence upon them. Both of them began to get very angry with me. They told me that they were sick listening to this "innocent lark" and demanded that I make a confession. The rougher of the two could hold his temper no longer and he started to scream and shout at me for having murdered his best friend, David Purvis. He came tearing across the room at me, stepping over the chairs, onto the table and over to where I was standing, roaring, "I'll kill the bastard! Let me at him!" several times. By the time he had reached me, his colleague had pushed me against the wall and was standing between us in an effort to save me. However, he was not fast enough, for several punches had already made their mark on my stomach.

The two of them resorted back to asking questions again, advising me to be careful how I answered them because I could be the cause of the whole affair boiling over again. After about five minutes I was told that I was being taken to another, larger room where they could have more space. This room was back up the corridor and faced the entrance to the interrogation block. Like all the other rooms, the door was painted blue and it had the number two on the front of it. Having entered the room with the two men, one of them locked the door from the inside. The room was much longer than the previous one and slightly wider. At a guess

I would say that it was about six metres long by about four metres wide. The room was furnished with a table, three tubular chairs, a small wastepaper bin about the size of a plastic bucket and the floor was covered with a dark brown carpet. Three of the walls were covered with the usual tiles while the outer wall was made of cream painted bricks. In this wall were two windows and below each window was a central heating radiator.

I was asked if I was prepared to make a statement about the terrorist activities which I was alleged to have taken part in. I said that I had no statement to make. I was then told that I would get to sit down on a chair when I was ready to make a statement. I was ordered to take up the awkward stance in which I was put during my first interview, keeping on my toes with my knees bent or flexed and my hands held straight out in front of me. I was made to stand in this position for about 15 minutes. While I was standing like this, the two detectives took off their jackets and ties and rolled up their shirt sleeves – then the fun really started. I was told that I would be lucky if I saw the light of day again without making a statement. One of the detectives said that the parents of Enniskillen would at last realise that their children were being taught by a murderer. He also said that my own children would never forgive me for being such a murdering bastard.

I was then ordered to start running on the spot. I did. I was told to lift my knees higher by the younger detective.

He shouted, "Higher, Higher, HIGHER." With each word he would shout louder. Then he would roar, "Faster, faster, FASTER." As my shoes were impeding my response to these commands, I was told to remove them. They were taken and literally kicked to the other end of the room. The detective who was still roaring at me to keep up the pace was by this time running on the spot with me. I was then told to run up and down the room from one end to the other. Every time I ran past either of the two men, I was kicked by them on the buttocks or the backs of the legs. At times I was able to avoid a kick by swerving past them. After about five or 10 minutes of this exercise I was again made to run on the spot. All this time both men were shouting and hurling abuse at me. For a rest I was allowed to stand in the now familiar awkward way.

I was then taken by the arms and flung from one detective to the other who was standing about five metres away. Neither man was too fussy as to how he caught me to throw me back, with the result that I did not know whether I was coming or going. Suddenly, in the middle of this throwing about, one of them would step to one side and I would go crashing against the wall with a loud thud. I found this to be quite a frightening experience as I did not know when one of them was going to step aside and let me hit the wall.

Again, for a rest I was made to stand in the awkward stance. While in this position the accusations came thick and fast. Each time I would deny any involvement. Several times I was slapped on the face and ears by both men for making these denials. The man who had punched me earlier for the murder of his friend was particularly vicious. He hit me several times with a closed fist on the stomach making me fall back against the wall. On several occasions I felt like being sick with the severity of the blows. This fact was noticed by the man who was administering them and he threatened, "If you get sick on the f****** floor, you'll get down on your f****** knees and eat it up again." Practically every phrase that he uttered was illustrated with a crude word of one kind or another. He had by far the foulest tongue of all the detectives I met in Castlereagh, although there were a few not too far behind him. His companion frequently used similar language but not to the extent which he did. The younger of the two did not like the way I spoke. He accused me of having too posh an accent to have come from the "bog," a reference to the rural district from which I originated. Several times he gave me a slap in the jaw for speaking too politely. He repeated things I said to him, imitating me in a mocking snobbish way, "Speak like a bog man," he would shout at me.

I was accused of teaching "Provo" songs to the boys in school. It was claimed that I taught songs in Irish to the boys and also a song called "The Men Behind the Wire." I explained that I trained the school choir to sing in Fermanagh Feis every year and I had taught them "The

Men Behind the Wire" because it was a pop song which had been number one in the Irish Top 10. I tried to explain that it was not a "Provo" song but a civil rights song. I received several punches in the stomach for my efforts. I was then made to run around the room singing "The Men Behind the Wire." The perspiration was flowing down my face like water in a shower by this stage.

I was again offered the chance of sitting down on a chair to make a statement, which I refused. This refusal seemed to make them even more desperate. I was again made to run on the spot, faster than before, lifting my knees higher. I then had to run up and down the room again. I was ordered to do 10 press ups, then 10 sit ups, then go back to running again. Every so often one of them would charge across the room at me and slam me up against the wall. Every bone in my body shook at this. On another occasion, one of them would punch me below the ribs in the stomach and land me on the floor gasping for breath. Immediately I would be pulled up again and made to run on the spot. At no stage during this interview was I allowed to stand up straight. I had to stand in the crouched position or keep running all the time.

In some ways this interrogation was equally tough on my interrogators as it was on me, for they continued to run on the spot and up and down the room with me. At one stage one of them remarked, "You are a fit f*****, O'Connor." I was impressed with the comment but not with the content.

He then asked did I drink or smoke and I replied that I did neither.

At this stage my entire clothing was saturated in sweat. As I ran on the spot my trousers were sticking to my legs. Because I was not lifting my legs high enough for them, they ordered me to remove my trousers, which I did. The older of the two told me to take off the rest of my clothes which he kicked up in the air several times until they reached the upper end of the room. He then commented on the "F****** set of it." The "it" being me. Referring to my private parts he said, "Look at the size of that to be the father of seven children. It's no wonder the balls are nearly worn off you, it's not worth my while kicking them in." Later he said, "Your wife must not be very fussy if she's satisfied with that."

I was made to go through all the previous exercises nude. I really felt sick and very embarrassed. I did not know what they were going to do with me next. I was kept naked for about half an hour, running, doing press ups, sit ups etc. Eventually my clothes were fired back to me and I was told to put them on again. They felt very cold and damp, yet soothing to my soaking body. Again, I got the offer to make a statement. I refused. As a result, it was back to running, sit ups, etc., just as before.

A new exercise was introduced. I was brought over to the radiator and made to stand facing it about two feet away. One of them caught me by the back of the neck and kept pumping my head up and down between my knees from a standing position. This exercise made me feel dizzy and sick. He kept on doing it, with the help of his fellow detective, about 20 times. Then it was back to press ups and sit ups again.

The brown tracksuit top which I was wearing was then taken from me and pulled down over my head. The arms of the garment were tied tightly around my neck and I was completely hooded. A hand came across my mouth from the outside of the tracksuit and another squeezed my nose, until I could no longer breathe. I could hear the older one shouting, "Choke the bastard, choke the bastard." I could not get even a short breath through the tracksuit. I found even my very stomach trying to come up into my throat until I could remember no more. I was sure that I was going to die. I must have fainted for maybe just a minute or two or perhaps for as long as five, I have no idea, but I came to with the same two detectives kicking me on the side and shouting at me to "Get the f****** up." Having struggled to my feet feeling very exhausted I was again made to stand in the crouched position.

They began to get really mad at this stage. I was called a "murdering Provo bastard" who had killed Constable Purvis. I was told that the murdered Purvis used to take the place of one of them on the rugby team in Enniskillen for matches that he could not manage to turn up to. They described to me in great detail the sorrowful scenes which took place at

Constable Purvis's funeral and particularly how his disabled father had cried bitterly at the graveside. I was blamed for this murder and told that I had not given Purvis a second chance and that the treatment which I was now getting was very trivial in comparison to that which poor Purvis had got.

One of them ran across the room screaming that he was going to kill me. This time I was not saved by his companion. I was punched in the stomach, slapped up against the wall and kicked over the floor. I was beginning to realise that my life was in real danger. I could clearly see my wife Pat and each of my seven children in my mind. I knew that if I died in these circumstances, my family would fully understand and not hold any grudge against me. I was convinced by now that I was getting near death and decided that I would not try to save myself from hitting the wall while they were throwing me from one to the other. In fact, I planned that I would dive against the brick wall and hit my head against it, hoping to perhaps fracture my skull but hopefully not kill myself. One way or another, I could end the torture without giving my interrogators the satisfaction of killing me. Thanks be to God I did not have to resort to this.

At another stage I was told by the older man that "Provo bastards" like me had been the cause of injuring him in an explosion. He then threatened to poke out my eyes with the finger of his left hand. He pointed it right up to my eyelashes. On another occasion the same man caught me by the right arm. He held it under his left upper arm and across his left wrist. Then with his right hand he pulled my right hand downwards, stretching it over his wrist until my hand began to separate from the wrist at the joint. The pain which ran through me was so severe that I could not even scream. I just leapt on my toes in agony. I thought that my wrist had been broken. In fact, he threatened to break my arm and it couldn't have been far off it. I was later amazed to note that this torturous act did not leave any mark or cause any swelling, however I will remember that thunderbolt of pain up my arm for the rest of my life.

The running on the spot, press ups, sit ups and running around the room continued. The demands for stepping up the speed increased as my movements became worse. For instance, during press ups I was kicked on the side if my body touched the ground. Another idea then came to their minds.

The wastepaper bin in the corner of the room was placed down over my head. All the papers, cigarette butts, and ashes fell over me and onto the floor. I was instructed by the younger detective to pick all the rubbish from the floor and put it back in the bin. I proceeded to scoop all the rubbish into a bundle and lift it in handfuls. I was quickly stopped from doing this and was told to pick up each piece of paper individually and put it back in the bin. Each cigarette butt had to be lifted in my mouth from the floor like a dog and also replaced in the bin. I got down on my knees and did exactly as I was told. I didn't mind doing this task as it meant that I was not being physically abused. However, it was a most demoralising activity and I felt no better than a dog.

During this lull in my interrogation, I could hear the same noises coming from at least one other room in the block. I would in fact guess that there could have been two other interrogations going on, judging from the sound. I could not however hear what was being said, but the screaming and shouting echoed throughout the building, and the walls and doors shook with the sound of people being thrown up against them.

I was by now feeling very tired and exhausted. I was finding it very difficult to stand in the crouched position on my toes while keeping my hands out in front of me. After a few minutes my legs would tremble and I would stagger about the floor, much to the enjoyment of the two detectives. Running on the spot was nearly impossible. To help me lift my legs higher I was again told to take off my trousers. They were soaking in sweat. They felt as if I had urinated in them. I was told to strip off the rest of my clothes. They were all saturated in sweat. Every piece of clothing, from my vest through to my shirt and right out to my brown jumper, felt as if they were just coming from a tub of water. I never experienced perspiration like it before or since; I did not think it possible for sweat to flow from the human body in the way I experienced.

When I finally dropped down my blue y-front underpants they noticed that I had soiled them. I had actually felt it happening when I was being pumped up and down. I explained this to them. However, this explanation was not enough. I had to keep telling them that I had soiled my pants until I said, "I shit myself." I then had to say that it was a kind of liquid shit, as they were not satisfied with the word diarrhoea. I then suffered a lot of verbal abuse for being such a "dirty wee bastard" as I was called. The younger one made a lot of capital out of the fact that here was a schoolteacher who spoke in a snobbish accent shitting himself. "If only the children could see you now," he said. "The only degree you have is a degree in shit." My soiled underpants were then lifted and put on top of my head. They hung down over my face with the soiled part between the legs directly in front of my nose. They were deliberately positioned like this by the coarser of the two men. I was then again ordered to stand in the awkward position. I was verbally abused for some time. On my right elbow I had an acne rash about a centimetre in diameter. This was soon noticed by my interrogators. I was asked what it was. I, feeling that they wanted me to express myself in the dirtiest terms possible, said that it was scurvy. The two of them then called me the dirtiest names imaginable for not having washed myself.

One of them, who had smoked numerous cigarettes, came over to me and pointed the lit end of the cigarette directly at the eyelash of my left eye. He said, "I'll burn the eyes out of you, you murdering Fenian bastard." I could feel the smoke of the cigarette making my eyes water. It was held there for a minute, then he held it right down to the point of my penis and told me that I would be the father of no more children. I waited, bracing myself for the sting of pain when he would touch me with the cigarette. It was a terrifying few seconds. However, thanks to the little humane instinct he had, he did not touch me with it.

During this period of the interview the door was knocked. I was pushed into a corner and the door was unlocked. Into the room came two more detectives dressed casually in shirts and trousers. I noticed that their shirt sleeves were rolled up and their collars were lying open. One of these men had a half empty bottle of Lucozade in his hand. He offered me a drink. I gladly accepted his offer but was then told that whenever I would sit down and write a statement, I could drink it all. The two newcomers then got a full run down of my interrogation. Great satisfaction was shown at the fact that I had "shit" myself. They laughed heartily at that. They even examined the underpants which were still on my head to see the evidence for themselves. I found it hard to keep from getting sick from the smell of the underpants hanging right in front of my nose. I thought that if I kept the detectives from knowing this, and they thought that they were having no effect, they might let me take them down from my head. A foolish assumption on my part. I was made to run around the room, do press up, sit ups etc., and run on the spot with the pants still on my head.

These two newcomers joined in the fun and also began kicking and punching me while calling me filthy names. At one stage the taller of the two lifted me above his head and spun me round in the air. He then threatened to throw me down on the table in wrestling style so as to break my back on the table; however, he thrust me out beyond the table and I landed on my back on the floor. I tried to grab his arms to save myself from the fall but it was to no avail. I landed on my back on the floor and I can clearly remember seeing the most beautiful shade of violet. I could see nothing else but this beautiful colour which seemed to stay for as long as I wanted it to remain, but I think it lasted about half a minute.

I was allowed to put my clothes back on again. The cool, damp feeling was wonderful. I was slapped in the face and punched for being too slow in dressing. I couldn't go any faster because the clothes were sticking to me. Before the two detectives left, the taller of the two hit me with a massive punch to the stomach which landed me back on the floor, against the wall. I felt as if I had been lifted through the air by the force of it. Breathing seemed impossible; I fought hard to regain my breath. Eventually I staggered to my feet taking short, quick breaths.

After the two newcomers left, I was again hooded as before in my tracksuit top. However, this time they did not keep their hands over my mouth and nose long enough for me to pass out. In fact, on this occasion, I felt like being violently sick and began trying to vomit. This may have been the cause of them letting me go.

About an hour after the two CID detectives left, they returned with fish suppers and beakers of water for the two men who were conducting my interrogation. To keep me occupied while they dined, the litter bin was again put over my head like before and I had to pick up every bit of paper piece by piece in my hand and lift the cigarette ends in my mouth. They all enjoyed watching me do this. I had got to the stage where mentally I did not care what they wanted me to do. I felt that when I was being punched that they were punching themselves and I wasn't feeling anything. I kept repeating the Sorrowful Mysteries to myself and now realised probably for the first time in my life what Christ had gone through. It gave me more satisfaction to feel a fraction of what he had suffered. I got the strength to carry on.

The two newcomers left again. The younger of my interrogators came to me with a beaker of water and asked if I wanted a drink. I was extremely thirsty and would have been delighted to have a drink. I said yes. He held out the beaker with some water in it for me to take from him. As I took hold of the beaker the detective hit my hand with his other hand and the water was spilled all over the floor. He started to curse and swear at me for thinking so little of the water he had given me. "Is that all you think of the drink that I gave you?" he shouted. He then tripped the legs from under me and ordered me to lick the water off the floor. I did as he ordered. The water stayed in bubbles on top of the dusty underfelt and under the circumstances it was good to get it. The coldness was refreshing to my mouth.

Throughout the entire procedure I was continually threatened that I would be killed. I was told that if ever I got out of Castlereagh, not that there was much chance of that, I would be shot by the UVF (Ulster Volunteer Force, a Protestant paramilitary organisation). They said that if the UVF didn't know about me that they would personally inform them. They went so far as to say that if the UVF hadn't killed me within six months of my release, they themselves would assassinate me. One of them said that he would drive the car while the other would fire the shot. They claimed that they were so convinced that I was a murderer that they could not in conscience let me live.

I told the detective who had been injured in an explosion that I could understand why he could become so emotionally involved during interrogation, but that I found it hard to excuse his colleague. I pleaded with them to see the folly of their actions but this only got me more abuse. I was told that they did not need any advice from a murdering bastard like me.

Finally, at the end of about six of the most frightening and cruel hours of my life, the two CID men put on their coats and ties. They told me that they were going to put me into a car and drive me to the top of the Shankill Road, which is a very militant Protestant part of Belfast, and drop me on the street. They brought me outside to do this, but as we passed the cell block I was brought up the steps and put back into my cell. They asked the uniformed policeman if I was the last and he said that I was. One of them came right into the cell with me and whispered into my ear, "I'll do you, Bernie."

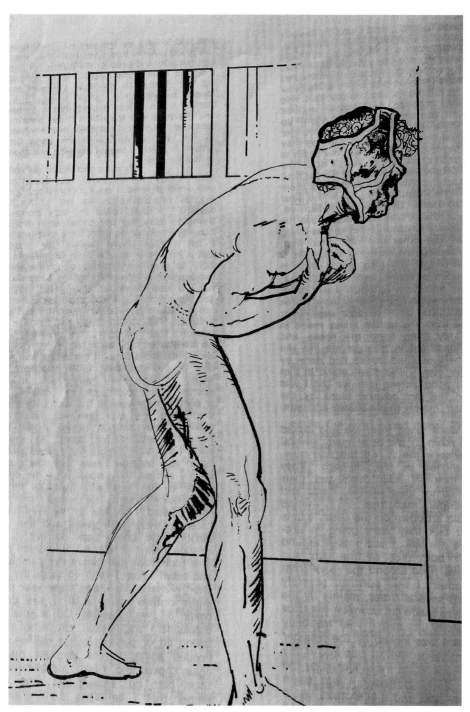

Artistic impression of me being stripped naked and wearing my underpants on my head
Fr Faul, 'Beating the Terrorist'

10

MY WIFE BACK HOME

Meanwhile, back in Enniskillen, my wife was doing all she could to help me. This is her account of what happened from lunch time on Thursday 20th January.

Just after lunch time, Agnes O'Reilly, a family friend, arrived to keep me company. I knew that Barney had not been in any political party since the days of the People's Democracy. Soon I had calls from all shades of opinion, and all were shocked and outraged at what had happened. As one local SDLP council member put it, "There is no one in this town whose movements are more public than Barney's, what with teaching, Boy Scouts and the driving school." Everyone was of the same opinion; something would have to be done. Hundreds of phone calls must have gone to Castlereagh. There was talk of a strike in the school where my husband worked. The Catholic population and some of the Protestants were up in arms. During Thursday from about 2.00 p.m. I phoned Castlereagh and asked about Barney. I was told that there was no change and no word of his release. Frank Maguire,

M.P., and his wife Philomena were a tower of strength to me. One of them phoned me every hour as well as phoning Castlereagh, just to let me know that they were thinking of me and were trying to do something to help to keep me going as I felt so helpless. I had never before realised that we in the six counties had absolutely no rights. My husband could be taken out of our home at 5.30 a.m. with no explanation given. No one outside of the RUC could get into Castlereagh to see if he was alive or dead. Barney's cousin, Gerry, and his wife, Agnes, decided to stay in the home with me for company and to look after the children. I was never alone except for one hour of the time Barney was away. On Thursday evening, when we started to say the family Rosary, one of the children asked me who would say Daddy's decade. All I could think of was how long it would be before their daddy would be home to say it. I also wondered if they would give him anything for his chest cold. I told the children that the police would soon realise the awful mistake that they had made and that their daddy would soon be home.

They kept asking, "Why did they take our daddy?"

What could I say when I didn't know myself? I just kept repeating: "It is a terrible mistake."

One of the girls, Sinead, aged seven, said that bad men with guns had taken Daddy and they must be in the IRA. I thought of the previous occasion when he had been held in the police station. I had been able to visit him as often as I could. It never entered my mind that he might be abused in Castlereagh. I was only worried that he would be out of his mind worrying about me and the baby and how lonely it must be for him without visitors. I went to bed at last and just lay there praying until it was time to get up again in the morning and phone Castlereagh.

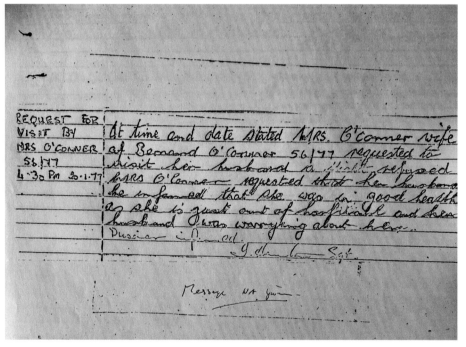

A copy of messages received from the logbook in Castlereagh. None were passed on to me

11

INTERROGATION 5

It was now between three and four o'clock in the morning of Friday 21st January and I was again back in my cell after experiencing the most horrific six hours of my life. I lay spread-eagled on the bed with exhaustion and distress. I was conscious of every inch of my body aching with soreness and pain. Even breathing caused pain and discomfort to my chest and stomach. And even though I had reached such a state of fatigue, sleeping was out of the question. My brain was very much alert and I couldn't stop thinking over everything that had just happened to me.

When I began to get my senses back a little, I realised that I needed to go to the toilet. I knocked the cell door and a uniformed constable opened it with the now familiar rattle of keys. He brought me to the toilet where I urinated. I then went over to the hand basin and turned on the cold tap. I put my head down sideways under the tap and began drinking. I will never forget the wonderful taste of that cool water. I drank and drank as much of it as I could.

Back in my cell I lay on the bed again, a little more composed than I had been. I literally cried to myself into the pillow when I realised what I had gone through. *Why had I been made to suffer like this? What makes men do to others as was done to me and what kind of animals are they?* More and more questions like these flashed through my mind. I was really frightened; I feared the dreaded footsteps back to my door to take me for another interrogation. I was convinced that I would not survive another session like the last. I thought for a long time about how near to death I had been. I knew that I had made the right decision not to sign a statement for something that I had no knowledge of, nor act, nor part in. I knew that to leave the world at this stage would have been a good thing: I thought of Enniskillen and all my friends; I thought of the school and of all the good times I had with the Scouts; I thought of my mother and sisters and the fact of joining my father in heaven; I thought especially of leaving my wife and seven wonderful children and never seeing them all again. I resigned myself eventually to believing that, if at a future interview I would be killed, it would be the will of God. I attempted to say the Rosary. Despite having to say several extra Hail Marys per decade to convince myself that I had said 10 for each Mystery, I eventually managed to get through it. This was a Rosary of thanksgiving said with real conviction for having survived the last ordeal. I was thankful for two reasons. Firstly, that God had given me the physical and mental strength to survive, and secondly, that I had the willpower to resist signing a statement for something which I had no act or part in. The Sorrowful Mysteries were a great source of strength to me. Throughout the interrogation I kept saying to myself, "Remember the second Sorrowful Mystery – the scourging of Christ at the pillar."

I spent the rest of the night thinking and praying. I kept repeating Rosary after Rosary and trying to reason out the whole precarious position I was in. I spent ages trying to figure out who could have framed me. I cast suspicion on everyone I worked with in the civil rights movement and the People's Democracy in Fermanagh during the active campaign in the late '60s and early '70s. I wondered if it was an act of jealousy on someone's part to land me in this situation. I tried to figure out who in Enniskillen could possibly be a member of the IRA and framed me to get himself out of the hands of the police. I could not think of one person who fit any of these suggestions. I wondered if it was a member of the police who wanted to get at me for my civil rights activities. I couldn't figure out the role of Inspector Harry Curry of the RUC in Enniskillen. Surely he knew that I was not involved in terrorist activities? Why did he allow my arrest? Or did the CID in Castlereagh act independently of the local police?

The rest of the night passed quickly and I was still no wiser at the end of it. The heat in the cell was very overpowering and made me feel very thirsty. At about six o'clock I knocked for a drink and to go to the toilet. Permission was granted.

I heard the changeover of the RUC personnel who guarded the cell blocks at seven o'clock that morning. I feared what the new day would bring. Every time the bolt of the cell block door snapped back, I trembled. I doubted my ability to withstand any more treatment similar to the previous night. I was feeling very sore. My legs were heavy and difficult to move and my back and shoulders had stiffened up. Looking right or left gave me sharp twinges of pain. I was feeling wretched both mentally and physically.

Sometime after seven o'clock that morning I was brought breakfast by a uniformed constable. Breakfast consisted of a fried egg, sausages, soda bread and tea. Food was the last thing I wanted to see. Although the meals were very well cooked and served, the sight and smell of it made me want to vomit. I sat down on the chair, took the paper plate on my knee and the beaker of tea on the floor beside my chair. I put two Tate and Lyle sugar cubes into my tea and kept two to suck later. I convinced myself that I needed to eat in order to give me strength; the problem was how to force myself to swallow it. I retched two or three times with every piece of food I put into my mouth, especially the egg, before I managed to chew it. To swallow it, I had to wash every mouthful down with a dash of tea. I got about halfway through my breakfast when my tea ran out and that was the end of my attempts to consume the rest. I thought it best not to tempt providence in case the whole lot came back up again.

After the leftovers were collected from my cell, I lay down on the bed again and waited for the inevitable. I said the Rosary again, begging God to help me in my next interrogation. I had not long to wait. At around ten o'clock the door knocking, bolt cracking and heavy marching began again. I was not the first person to be taken out but either the third or fourth. I was dying to find out who the others were. From the cavalcade of cars to Castlereagh the previous morning from Enniskillen, I was curious to know who was in them. I had asked the policeman who had brought me my breakfast that morning who else from Enniskillen was in here and he informed me that he was not permitted to tell me. In a way it was like getting another slap in the face. I was sorry that I had even bothered to ask him.

When my cell door opened, I was told to come out. I was again brought up to the table where a plain-clothes detective was waiting for me. He signed the usual forms before escorting me down to the interrogation block. I was brought back to the same room where I had endured that long, agonising interview until three or four that morning. I had not seen the two detectives who were to interrogate me before. One was dark, wire-haired and sturdy. The other detective was a little taller than his companion. He had a thin face and a rather sharp nose. He spoke with a pronounced Belfast accent.

When the interview began, I was told to stand about two feet from the wall. I was to keep looking out of the window which had frosted glass. During the questioning, the smaller of the two men kept walking around behind me, squeezing between me and the wall. If I looked to the right or left at any time, he shouted at me in a very aggressive way, "Weren't you told to keep looking out the f****** window!" With a slap to the face or a punch to the stomach he would inform me, "You'll soon learn to do what you're f****** told in here."

I must add that I was allowed to stand in an upright position at all times. I soon discovered though, that both these CID men were very short tempered. The smaller, dark-haired detective had two very vicious ways of trying to hurt me. He continually punched the back of my skull with his closed fist until I believe his knuckles began to hurt him. He held my forehead in his other hand so as to keep my head from jerking back as he punched away. After the first four or five sets of punches my head went numb. My eyes became bleary and at times I could see nothing else but pink, white and green rings moving towards me. The other brutal habit which this man had was that he stood in front of me and slapped my face and ears with open hands, both right and left, in quick succession. The other detective punched me regularly in the stomach and prodded me with rigid fingers in my chest. I felt that his fingers were going right through me. With the force of each punch, I fell back against the wall. Of course, it didn't take much to knock me over at that stage, but nevertheless this man's punches were very bitter. The more I insisted on my innocence, the more wicked both men became. At one stage during this interview the smaller, dark haired man worked himself up into such a rage slapping my face and ears from left to right that he went white in the face. He told me that he was leaving the room for a break and if I had not begun writing statements by the time he got back, he would take me to within "an inch of my life."

He returned after about 15 minutes but abused me to much the same extent after he returned. The other detective only hit me in the stomach. When he got worked up he would come right up to my right ear and scream into it at the top of his voice, "You're a f****** murderer, You're a f****** murderer." He would shout this nine or 10 times. He would then ask me to repeat back to him what he had said. I refused to do so. He would then repeat it again after accusing me of being "f****** deaf". If I had repeated back to him "I'm a f****** murderer," I would in fact have been making a verbal statement incriminating myself. Indeed, a verbal statement like that could get a person 30 years in Long Kesh. After being put under a lot of pressure to repeat the above, I finally said to him "You told me that I'm a murderer but you know very well that I am not." Several times I was told by both men that I deserved to be shot and that they would see to it if I ever got out of there.

In the middle of this three-or-four-hour interview, another unknown detective came breezing into the room.

He was a tall man, well-groomed wearing a rust-coloured three quarter-length coat. He came right over to me smiling and announced, "We got your mate this morning O'Connor, we shot your mate." I was very confused at this. I began wondering who had been shot in Enniskillen. This new detective went on to elaborate. He said that my fellow Provo from Castlederg, a Mr McHugh, had been shot dead at the side of his lorry while going to work that morning. I was told that I was in a similar position to McHugh, that I would be shot too if I ever got out of Castlereagh. He told me that in no way would the police let a Provo godfather like me be free to roam about; I would have to be shot like McHugh. He said that McHugh was the godfather in Castlederg and that his schoolteacher wife who had found him would have plenty to write to the papers about now. I gathered from his comments that Mrs McHugh used to write Republican-type letters to the papers. I explained that I was not nor ever was a "Provo" and that I did not know of a Mr McHugh in Castlederg. I was pushed back against the wall and told to wipe the smile off my face by the detective who then put his fist under my chin and began stretching my head up against the wall. He kept this up until he raised me up off my toes off the ground. He then let go quickly and I shrank in a heap against the wall. I thought that my neck was broken. He told me that no one smiles at him and gets away with it. He complimented the other two on the good job they were doing and on leaving the room told me that I would be seeing him later.

During the last half hour or so of my interview with both these men I was allowed to sit down at the table. One of them produced a little green folder from his briefcase. He started giving me a lecture on the seriousness of taking a life and the suffering it caused to relatives – all of which I was in total agreement with. He placed the little green folder in front of me on the table and told me to open it. Inside was a black and white photograph of two or three mutilated bodies lying on white slabs in the mortuary. Each body had a label attached to the foot or leg or whatever limb was left of it. These were identification labels. I was told to look at this photograph and comment on it. I looked at it and then told them that I could not agree with such terrible crimes. I was then told that two of the bodies in the photograph were those of the UDR (Ulster Defence Regiment) and that I was responsible for their murder. I thought that they had gone mad. I told them that they were bound to know that this was not true. I asked them to contact the RUC in Enniskillen and that they would tell them how I spent my time. I said that it was common knowledge to the Enniskillen Police that I taught from nine to half past three every day. I gave driving lessons with the B & H Driving School from four p.m., passing the RUC station 20 or 30 times each evening. I helped out as a part-time youth leader in St Michael's Youth Club Enniskillen at least four nights a week and as a Boy Scout Leader two nights per week.

I then asked them where or when did I get time to carry out or even plan all these terrible acts of violence? I might as well have been talking to the wall. Both men were adamant that I was the right man and I was going to have to face the consequences. They then went on to lecture me on how they dealt with other "intelligent bastards" in Castlereagh and how they eventually cracked them just like the way I would be. I found it very hard to concentrate on what they were saying to me during these long lectures. I began thinking that I was back in my class at school, and I was teaching the boys how to find the area of a space. I used the little wire-grilled air vent in my cell as a problem for the boys. The grill was about 20 centimetres in size, the wire bars in it crisscrossed diagonally leaving a mesh of about one and a half centimetres wide. I was trying to get the boys to find out how many squares were in the grill and what was its area. I was away in a world of my own when I was suddenly brought to my senses with the words, "There's no point talking to the bastard, sure he's away in a trance." A swift slap to the side of the face soon brought me back to my senses all right. I must have been asked a question and didn't answer it so they realised that I wasn't listening to them. Again, the lecturing went on. Finally, at about one o'clock or so I was finally brought back to my cell for lunch. It was the end of another very tough, gruelling three hours and I still had not signed a statement, much to their disgust.

The one thing that I noticed about all the interviews so far was that one of the detectives during each interview wrote pages and pages of data on the interview. I would have loved to have read them. All these pages went into my file, which was by now getting very thick.

12

INTERROGATION 7

Another gruelling interrogation session over and I was now trying to relax on my bed in the cell. My brain was working like a cement mixer, everything very jumbled up and confused. I tried to reason out one thing after another but my concentration was now practically nil. I tried to recall what the last two detectives had said to me and compare it with all that the other interrogators had said up to now, to see if I could piece together any bits of information which might help me to discover why there had been another interrogation so quickly. I ached all over and with the peripheral vision of my left eye I could see the outline of my swollen left ear. I tried to say another Rosary as I was convinced that the only thing which kept me sane was prayer. About every second or third Hail Mary my mind wandered off on a tangent. At this stage it would be enough to say that I made an attempt to say a thanksgiving Rosary.

When I had been back in my cell for a short time a

policeman brought me a beaker of water and two Penbritin capsules. I drank all the water and asked for a refill, which I was given. I had drunk what seemed like gallons of water by now. Every time that I was allowed out to the toilet, I drank three or four beakers of water. I had lost so much sweat during interview and the central heating in the cell was so hot and exhausting that my body was drying up, so I had to keep drinking and drinking.

Lunch arrived and it consisted of potatoes, fish and peas. Again, I had to begin the battle to eat. Despite almost being sick several times I managed, thanks to the beaker of water, to eat most of the meal.

To think about my wife and children back home made me feel very lonely. My Adam's Apple thickened in my throat and tears found their way down my face and into my ears while lying on my bed. I therefore tried not to think about them and attempted to concentrate on what was going on instead. I was bleary eyed and seeing coloured images in my eyes from being senseless and from lack of sleep. However, despite not having slept, there was not the slightest chance of my dozing off with the way my brain was buzzing. I resorted back to prayer and another Rosary of preparation. After what I had gone through during the previous two interviews, I began to doubt that there was a God in existence at all. Nevertheless, I felt that the only help I could get in the circumstances was from God, if there was one, so I felt that I had nothing to lose by praying and if anything, all to gain. Another effort was made, and I chalked up another Rosary.

For the next three hours or so, I was interrogated in room four. This was a similar room to the previous ones and furnished likewise. My interrogators however were different in every respect to the others. I recognised one of them as a detective who had looked into the interrogation room with a colleague the previous afternoon when I was being interviewed. He was of slim build, bald with grey hair round the sides of his head and he was very sharp featured. The other man had dark hair going grey in places.

They told me that I could sit down and talk to them and that they were not there to abuse or threaten me but to convince me to have sense. One man did most of the talking. He began by saying how sorry he was to see an intelligent schoolteacher like myself involved with an organisation like "PIRA." It took me sometime to realise that PIRA stood for the Provisional IRA. During other interviews the IRA were referred to as the "Provos" but now it was PIRA. Deep concern was expressed for my wife and seven pitiful children who were now going to be left without a father for the rest of their childhood at least. It was explained that I had taken a decision and I would now have to face the consequences and though the terrible crimes in which I had been involved were things of the past, that did not take away the guilt. I would have to be a man and somehow face up to reality and confess my part in these crimes. One of the detectives in particular gave me no chance to contradict him or to explain to him how wrong he was. I tried to tell him numerous times at the start that he was talking to the wrong man, but he just went on and on. I had to sit and listen to it all. He eventually got around to talking about the civil rights campaign and the part I had played in it. He was very well versed in the speeches I had made and the demonstrations I had taken part in. He told me that he agreed with the civil rights campaign and that it was important for it to succeed. Discrimination existed in jobs and housing in Northern Ireland, indeed it even existed in the RUC. He went on to elaborate that thanks to Arthur Young, the RUC were now one of the finest and most impartial forces in the world. I felt like saying, being in the situation in which I found myself, I could contradict that statement but I did not have the nerve. This same detective proceeded to take his logic a step further. He noted that after the civil rights campaign had more or less ended in 1971-72, I had dropped out of all activities. Whilst most of the political leaders like John Hume, Austin Curry and Ivan Cooper had previously been involved in the CRA., I did not follow that pattern. As I did not turn to politics, he suggested that I had gone underground, as no one with such deep convictions as I had could have dropped out of political life altogether.

At this stage he gave me a chance to explain. I told him that the biggest mistake ever made by the leaders of the CRA movement was to get involved in politics. It divided the people right down the middle. I explained that the struggle for basic civil rights in this country was as big an issue today as it was then. I pointed out that England's policy in relation to the Irish was always one of "divide and conquer" and that is exactly what they did to the civil rights movement. People like Curry, Fitt, Devlin, Hume and Cooper allowed themselves to be wooed round the table where big jobs were offered to them in the executive and they fell for it. I went on to explain that the people of the street campaigns allowed themselves to be conned into a situation of:

1. Backing the misguided politicians.
2. Supporting militant organisations.
3. Being disillusioned with the whole dirty business and giving up.

I said that like most of the people of Fermanagh, I had resorted to option three. I added that I blamed the politicians for allowing themselves to be brought off the streets by England, because if the struggle had gone on, people would not have backed the militants to such an extent out of frustration from being let down. I, out of disgust at seeing the Currys and Fitts etc., using the civil rights to feather their own nests in politics, withdrew from being involved with the attitude that I would not be used by anyone.

My efforts were all in vain for my interviewer was still not convinced. He was still adamant that I was involved in acts of terrorism. In fact, he became very specific as to which particular incidents he wanted me to admit to taking part in and even the actual degree of participation I had in the crimes. There were the two murders of policemen in particular, which he wanted me to confess to. He said that he knew that I wasn't involved in pulling the actual trigger, because I was far too intelligent for that, but I was the brains behind the killings. He claimed that I was "the godfather", who was sending out young men to do the crimes and he thanked God that at last they had caught up with me. He then went off on a long lecture about murder and quoted case after case of murder victims which he had to deal with. Two sets of photographs of mutilated bodies were then produced from a briefcase. One set was in a green folder which the two previous detectives had shown me and the other was in a blue folder with other photographs of horrific crimes. One of the booklets was placed on my knee and I was told to keep looking at the gruesome pictures. I was ordered to not look away but to just keep my eyes on them. I did so for four or five minutes. Another page would be turned up for me to view more horrific pictures. At this stage the inspector was sitting on the edge of the table right in front of me and looking down over me. He said that no normal man could look at those photographs and not show some signs of emotion. He looked straight into my eyes and said, "O'Connor, you have the cold eyes of a killer."

I just stared straight back at him in disgust at this

comment, which was repeated several times during the remainder of the interview. I felt so insulted that I could not answer him. In fact, I felt that there was no point in answering him as he would refuse to listen anyway.

Again, during this interview, like during the interrogations on Thursday afternoon, I was accused of having bought my home with the proceeds of an armed robbery in Enniskillen. As before, I reacted very quickly and positively, denying the allegation. The other man, who spent most of his time writing and who very seldom spoke, asked me why I reacted in such a way to being accused of receiving the stolen money. He said that he had watched me being accused of all sorts of crimes, even murder, and the only thing that had stirred a reaction in me was this allegation. I explained to him that I had numerous positions in the parish organisations involving public fundraising activities and I was always one to make sure that such money should be accounted for to the last penny. Hence, I explained my annoyance at being accused of being involved in any sort of financial fiddle or theft. I then went further to explain to them that thanks to a 100% mortgage from the Colonial Mutual, arranged through my teachers' union, I was able to purchase my home. I invited them to make a few telephone calls to clarify the problem. Needless to say, no phone calls were made.

Another accusation which they made against me was that I attended the PIRA Wolfe Tone parade in Kildare in 1976 at Bodenstown. I explained to them that on the date in question, which was on the second Sunday in June, I attended the National Executive Meeting of the Catholic Boy Scouts in 19 Herbert Place in Dublin. I also invited them to check this out by either phoning Scout Headquarters in Dublin and asking them to furnish them with a copy of the minutes of that meeting or request the Garda (Irish Police), with whom they had boasted on several occasions to be in close contact with, to furnish them with a copy of the minutes of that and many other meetings that I attended in Dublin.

The bald-headed inspector kept on at me for not showing remorse at seeing the photographs. He kept up his "cold eyes of a killer" comment until I could take it no more. I finally tried to defend myself. I told him that black and white glossy photographs like those, although horrible looking, would not cause the upset he seemed to expect. I said that if they were in colour or even in slides or film, they would have more of an effect. I suggested that he should show them to people responsible for such crimes and it might have some effect on them. I also suggested that he should take such film along to the upper classes in grammar and secondary schools so that they might act as a deterrent to young people getting involved in such crimes. Although he agreed with me the other inspector said that he could not do that because the relatives of the bodies in the photographs would be annoyed at their deceased being shown freely around the country.

At the end of the interview, I again tried to reason with them. I told them that I was being accused of being a murderer and having "the cold eyes of a killer", but really deep down they know that I never was involved in such crimes. I will never forget the inspector's answer: "Whether a man is guilty or not, we have to say those things anyway."

On being put back into my cell, I was told by both men that if I wanted to meet them again to discuss any problems, they would always make themselves available. It was nice to part on friendly terms for a change.

13

INTERROGATION 8, 9, 10

At around 5.30 on Friday afternoon, I had a visitor to my cell. He was a uniformed sergeant of the RUC; he informed me that my wife was on the phone and that she was concerned about me. She wanted me to know that both she and the children were well and for me not to worry about them. The sergeant also said that my wife wanted to know if I wished to see my family doctor from Enniskillen. He went on to elaborate further, "If you want to see a doctor in here you have to ask for him yourself, your wife or no one else can have him sent in."

I replied "yes" that I would love to see my own doctor and thanked him for his help. On parting he announced that he would tell my wife of my request.

I was feeling really sorry for myself at this stage. My ears were badly swollen, particularly the left, and they were burning hot all the time. My shoulders neck and head had gone very stiff and were sore to move. The muscles in the backs of my legs were aching and causing me great discomfort when I had to walk.

I ate most of my tea when it came. I also had two Penbritin tablets, drank another few beakers of water and then I said the usual two semi-conscious Rosaries before being taken from my cell for another interview at around seven o'clock.

I was brought to room five by a young detective sergeant of about 30 with brown, wavy hair. He was about 5 feet 10 in height and wore a navy pinstriped suit. He told me to take a seat beside the table. Within minutes another detective came into the room. He was a Chief Superintendent of Crime Squad and he had come into the first interrogation session I had that morning. This time he carried a black solid frame attaché case. He removed his overcoat and folded it across a chair. He then opened his case which was on the table in front of me and took from it a bulging file which he threw down on the side of the table. He took a pad and a black HMSO Biro from the case and placed them in front of me. He left the case on the floor and both men sat down. One of them was seated directly in front of me and the other was on my right. The younger of the two began writing notes to put in my file as all the other interviewers had done. The usual preliminary questions were asked again. Name, age, address, wife's name, children's names and ages. At every interview up until now these exact details had been taken; it all seemed rather pointless. The older of the two placed the Biro on the pad in front of me.

"There's going to be no more messing," he said. "Pick up that pen and start writing." I refused. I then got a long lecture about wasting time and not having sense and, like the other interrogators, he explained the importance of keeping myself in prison for a few months so as to avoid being assassinated by the UVF.

I was told that there was no way I could avoid being killed by the Protestant paramilitaries if I was released. In fact, if they could not get me, they would kill either my wife or one of my children or go so far as to blow up my home. The only way I could avoid this was by making a small statement incriminating myself, irrespective of whether I was guilty or not. This, I was told, could be the means of saving myself, or indeed more importantly, my wife and children. The older man did most of the talking during this interview while the other did all the writing and made the odd back up comment.

Some of the statements were then read from my file. These were allegedly made by either some other suspect under interrogation or an informant. I was told at first that they were made by a person from Enniskillen who had qualms of conscience over the terrible crimes committed in the area and wanted to clean up the place once and for all by getting people like me removed from society.

The statements generally read as follows:

"I went to O'Connor and gave him the numbers of police cars and the times I saw them."

"Bernard O'Connor told me that another policeman would have to be shot so I told him I would."

"I drove behind O'Connor's car. His car was being used as a scout car to bring explosives to Enniskillen."

Page after page of these types of allegations were read to me.

The strange factor in relation to all the statements was that my name, as quoted by the fictitious "I" person was always Bernard O'Connor, yet all my friends, and in fact most people in Enniskillen, call me either Bernie or Barney O'Connor but seldom Bernard. This was the first thought which struck me as the statements were being read to me. Even the RUC in Enniskillen call me "Bernie." Both men tried to convince me that this "I" person was very reliable and they fully believed him. They even went so far as to threaten to bring him to Castlereagh where I would be confronted face to face with him. I told them to do that, but they refused because they said that a top Provo like me would be able to have their key witness "dealt with." On being asked to even name him, they again stated that they would be putting his life at risk by letting me know him. The idea they kept giving me was that I was the "godfather" figure who held a high rank in the IRA.

Their approach drifted gradually to a situation where they were catering for my welfare by getting me a prison sentence to protect me from the UVF, all the while trying to incriminate me in a murder charge. I was told that criminals must always repent and that applied to me too. All the fictitious "I" statements were read to me over and over again. There were 15 to 20 of them. In some way or other they were accusing me of being involved in four murders, about 20 explosive offences and two armed robberies. This may seem amusing now, but I can assure you that at the time there was nothing to be amused about. I was told that I would have to write a statement for each allegation. I kept appealing to them to try and understand my innocence. The Chief Inspector began a long lecture on what is meant by cooperation in custody. He explained to me that when a detective stands up in court and tells the judge that a person was uncooperative in custody, the judge would give a very severe sentence to the suspect. However, if a suspect was termed as being cooperative in custody, he then would impose the smallest sentence possible. He continued to tell me that in my case a sentence for any of the murder charges in which he alleged I was involved, would result in a stipulated life sentence of 35 years. If I was to hurry up and not waste time and write a statement confessing to murder, I would be termed by the CID as having been cooperative and so get an ordinary life sentence with any stipulation. In fact, such a life sentence would be of 14 years duration and as the crime committed was before 1976, the sentence would be halved. A further remission of good behaviour would take a further one third off the rest so I would only have to do five years. To avoid having to face a number of murder charges at all, I was offered a deal. The file was opened and I was offered a choice of any of the offences. I was told that if I wrote a statement confessing to any of the statements that the fictitious "I" gave them they would be totally satisfied and all this would end. I was told to pick the least incriminating of them. As a result, they would use their influence with the judge so that I would get the least possible sentence. And this led to another long lecture because I refused emphatically to write a statement as I was innocent.

Now there was no other option for them. I was going to be the cause of my own destiny and spend 35 years in prison. They asked me to think back 35 years and imagine what life was like then and then I was asked to imagine what the next 35 years was going to be like in the world and all the changes. They painted a very primitive picture of life as it had been 35 years ago. They compared the very inadequate living standards and the poor educational facilities with today's affluent society. They referred to the scientific developments of the past and prophesied even more elaborate inventions in the future. I was informed that I would spend 35 years in prison with maybe a day's release on compassionate grounds for my mother's or sister's funeral, or perhaps to attend the weddings of some of my children. After 35 years I would not be able to adjust to modern society. I would be an old, bent, grey haired man with a stick who would end up in a mental home for the remainder of my days – that is, if I lived that long. They said that my family would not even want to know me then. They would never forgive me for having deserted them during their childhood. I found this discussion particularly distressing as I was very closely attached to my children. I was listening to them.

I again refused to sign any statements, although I was beginning to believe that I was going to be charged with any number of the offences even without my signature. I was also concerned with the influence they claimed to have with the judiciary in committing me to prison for the rest of my life. At this stage, the Superintendent, who was annoyed with my non-cooperation, took the pad and pen from in front of me and said that if I was not going to make a confession, he would have to write a statement for me himself. I will never forget the words with which he began the statement.

"I, Bernard O'Connor, wish to clear the following murder off my chest."

He went on to write how I had set up a policeman to be shot dead in Belmore Street, Enniskillen, and how I had passed on the details to the Provos, who then drove through the town and shot the policeman in question. At the end of the statement, they then wrote words to the effect that the statement had been made at a certain time and that it had been made freely and voluntarily and without duress. He then put it in front of me to sign; I completely refused. He took the pad again and told me that one unsigned statement might not be enough to fully influence the judge, but a second one should convince him. He commenced a second statement which involved me in another murder. He concluded this statement in a similar way to the first.

I could feel myself getting frightened because he was so convincing and my ability to concentrate and think straight was affected because I was suffering from exhaustion and lack of sleep. I was, in a way, getting brainwashed.

The Superintendent said that it would not stick in his throat to present these statements in court and swear that they had been made voluntarily by me in custody but I had refused to sign them. He informed me that the judge always takes the word of a detective in court and my words would not be listened to. The fact that I would deny these statements in court would show the judge that I was not an honest and reliable witness and therefore I would get a life sentence stipulated for 35 years. By this stage I was quite convinced that I was going to be charged in court for the two murders. Both detectives spent some time explaining to me that although I did not commit the murders, the two statements showed my involvement in them, so I was as guilty in the eyes of a judge as if I had committed the actual crime. I tried to reason with them and appealed to their conscience to realise that what they were doing was wrong. I was told that it was I who had the guilty conscience and even if it meant perjuring themselves to get me sentenced their minds would be clear. They told me that this was nothing new for them. I again and again protested my innocence but I was totally ignored.

Being now more convinced than ever that I was going to face the court, I requested to see my solicitor. I was told by the Superintendent that no solicitors get into Castlereagh, but that I would see one in court which would take place in Enniskillen on either Saturday evening or Monday morning.

Several times during the next hour's interrogation I was asked to sign the two murder statements and each time I refused. Again and again it was pointed out to me the consequences of being uncooperative in custody, and how this was a very stubborn and stupid attitude for "an intelligent school teacher."

At least two other detectives took part in this interview. They tried to give me a bit of fatherly advice and encourage me to set my mind at rest by signing a statement confessing to my alleged terrorist activities. I don't think that any of these detectives were aware of the fact that the two murder statements were written by the Superintendent. These two detectives did not threaten or abuse me. They seemed to be there to softly advise me to cooperate and sign statements.

The Superintendent and his partner returned at about eleven o'clock that night. I was in this interrogation room from after seven o'clock without a break. They told me that they had come back to give me a second chance. Their approach was different to begin with. "After all," the older man began, "what satisfaction do you think we get out of putting the father of seven children in prison for 35 years?"

The two statements were then produced from the black briefcase and put down on the table in front of me. I was then told of a deal which they would be prepared to make with me. In a very concerned tone of voice, the Superintendent invited me to tear the two murder statements into tiny bits, on condition that I was prepared to make a statement involving myself in the fictitious "I" confessions. Both men went to great lengths to point out to me that they wanted to do this as a great favour to me. Such a small confession would only get me a very small sentence. Of course, if I was not prepared to accept the deal, I would leave them with no alternative but to use the murder statements. I told them that I was not prepared to as much as touch the two statements, never mind tear them up. I refused, by now rather hesitantly, to make or sign a statement. I told them that I couldn't trust them to make a deal even if I wanted to. I stressed that I was never going to make a statement admitting to something that I never did. Both men tried to assure me that they were men of integrity and they would definitely keep their word. Having two fictitious murder statements held over me did not convince me of their integrity. I don't know where I was getting the strength from to hold out.

The younger detective took the pad in his hand and told me that he would write the statement for me. I was going through mental hell. I was beginning to believe them but the word "brainwashing" kept coming into my mind. I again got the strength to protest my innocence.

I got the common-sense lecture again and they both read statements to me from the file. They were even picking statements for me. The young detective wrote a statement involving me in a work of mercy, bringing an injured man to hospital. Again, I refused to sign it, as it was not true. He started to write another statement trying to involve me in a robbery. I told him he was wasting his time.

By this stage I was totally exhausted. They referred to the fact that I was not eating very well since I arrived in Castlereagh. The Superintendent sent the younger man out to get a fish supper and something to drink. While he was away, the Superintendent spent a long time trying to convince me that he was only doing his best to help me. He had found out from Enniskillen how helpful I was in the community and how dedicated I was to my family. He assured me he would do his best to have me back in Enniskillen as soon as possible.

After about 20 minutes his colleague arrived back with fish suppers in newspaper and two cans of Fanta. He also had three white plastic beakers. The fish suppers were shared out among the three of us and the two tins of Fanta were poured equally into the three beakers. I enjoyed the fish which was very palatable. I enjoyed the Fanta even more. In fact, the break gave me time to get control of myself and realise how I was being brainwashed by them. I would definitely not sign statements about something I didn't do. I convinced myself.

After supper it was back to business. The problem they had was to get me to select an offence and make a statement. I was asked would I be the "look out" for the bomb at the White Star Bar, or lend my car to ferry explosives to the B and M Motors, or do lookout for the robbery at McDermott's Supermarket, etc. etc. The list of alternatives seemed endless. I kept refusing to involve myself in any of their offers, so they quickly went back to the two murder statements. It was either going to be murder or an involvement of my choice.

"Surely it doesn't take an intelligent schoolteacher long to decide between these two options?" I was again asked.

I suggested to them that I was totally confused and perhaps they would let me go back to my cell for some sleep. I told them that I could no longer understand what they were saying so I was going to sign nothing. They told me they would be back with me first thing in the morning and during the night I was to decide what I was going to sign. When he was picking up his papers and the file the Superintendent lifted the two murder statements and, putting them in his breast pocket, told me that I would be able to tear them up in the morning if I signed a statement for him. When he got as far as the door, he turned and came back to me at the table. He took the two murder statements from his pocket and said, "Here, write on each of these that you refuse to sign them."

As tired as I was, I told him that I was writing nothing on those statements. I was having nothing to do with them. He put them back inside his breast pocket and left the room. I was brought back to my cell by the other man at some time after 2am.

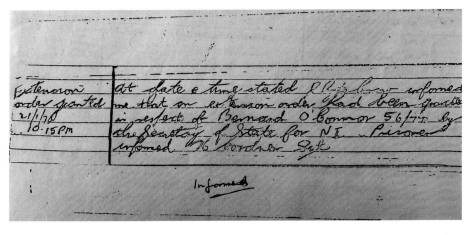

This was one message they made sure to let me receive – an extension of another five days of interrogation

14

INTERROGATION 11

On arrival back at my cell I was given two Penbritin tablets by a uniformed policeman. He asked if I wanted a drink of milk to wash them down and I, being very fond of milk, was delighted to accept. I spent most of the night in my cell condemning myself for being so stupid. When I had time to lie on the bed and think of how they were attempting to trick me into signing statements about being involved in terrorism I could feel myself getting very hot in the face and neck. I am sure that my blood pressure rocketed. The fact that I had even considered these "deals" at all made me realise that I must be losing control of my senses. My big problem was how to get out of the mess I was in. I had prayed very hard up until then, but I prayed more that night than I had ever done before in my life.

At times during the night, I resigned myself to the fate of signing a statement. On other occasions I convinced myself that I must refuse to sign anything. I even tried examining the walls and air vent to see if I could break out and run away from it all. Not a thing could I do. To make matters worse I was feeling very stiff and sore all over. I had been sitting in the same spot during the last interrogation for at least seven or eight hours and I had also remained seated during the afternoon session. This total lack of movement had tightened up all my muscles. I was particularly sore along my shoulders and up the back of my neck and head. My ears seemed to be on fire. My legs were very painful to straighten out especially along the balls of my feet. I was coughing a lot, which caused mouthfuls of green phlegm to come up. I was very depressed.

I decided that I would try to sleep. I undressed and got under the bedclothes and tried to get my brain relaxed in order to sleep. I was even foolish enough as to literally try counting sheep. My ability to count at this stage was a major problem. Counting 10 Hail Marys for each decade of the Rosary was now virtually impossible but trying to concentrate on counting sheep was even worse. I abandoned the idea after a couple of attempts. Sleep was out of the question. I felt that the light in the cell was too bright to sleep, the cell was too hot, the noise of the fan blowing hot air was too annoying and so on. I found 101 reasons why I could not sleep. Of course, the main one was that my brain just would not settle. I felt so very mentally alert.

Several times during the night as I lay there in bed, I heard the policeman on guard coming to the little spy glass in the cell door to have a look in at me. I would then lie quite still and pretend that I was asleep. I heard the usual change of police personnel at seven that morning. Shortly after that I was brought breakfast. Despite efforts to eat the fried egg and sausages, I left most of it.

As far as I remember it was on this Saturday morning after breakfast that I had a visitor to my cell. He was a uniformed policeman with bad news for me. He informed me that as I had been arrested under Section 12 of the Prevention of Terrorism Act, my term of detention was being extended from two days to seven. Permission to do this had been granted by the Secretary of State for Northern Ireland.

I was not surprised at this latest bit of news because I understood that Section 12 meant up to seven days detention anyhow. I was not aware that after the first two days permission for a further five days was necessary.

Every move in the cell block that morning frightened me. I dreaded the meeting again with the two detectives I had the previous night. I had convinced myself by then to refuse to sign any statement involving myself in terrorism. I was innocent and I was going to stand up for my rights irrespective of the consequences. Nevertheless, I feared the next interview. Several other detainees were taken from their cells that morning before I was. One of the names called aloud was "Maguire." As "Maguire" is such a common name in Enniskillen, I wondered which Maguire he could be, if he happened to be from Enniskillen. My mind jumped from one Maguire to another, but I could not figure out which family he might be from. Eventually I dismissed the idea from my mind by pointing out to myself that there are Maguires from all parts of the north and he could be from anywhere.

Eventually my cell door was opened and I was taken for interrogation. My first two interrogators were the dreaded pair from the night before. All the relevant documents were taken from the Superintendent's case and put on the table. The other detective armed himself with a pen and a foolscap writing pad which had the green RUC crest on the top of each page. After going through the usual preliminary formalities of an interview, detailing name, date of birth, address, wife's name, full Christian names of children etc., I was asked if I had thought over the proposition. I told him that I had. He then asked me which statement I had picked. I explained to him that I was never involved in any acts of terrorism of any kind and having spent hours considering their deal, I had decided to face the consequences and not to make or sign any statement.

My two interviewers could not believe their ears. I was asked if I was serious. I was told by the older one that I had to make a statement because my friends were singing like birds about me. He told me that four others from Enniskillen were in Castlereagh and that they were telling them everything. I asked him what he meant. He asked if I knew anyone by the name of Thomas Vincent Maguire. I told him that I knew a youth of that name who was a member of the Boy Scouts. He then produced a number of photostatic handwritten statements from his case. He asked if I recognised the handwriting. Each page was signed at the bottom by Thomas Vincent Maguire. I was not allowed to read the statements, but I was told that they were all about me. The Superintendent went on to tell me that Curry, Martin and McDonagh were all writing statements about me. I knew that this could not be possible because, apart from being involved with two of these young men as Scouts, I had no association with them during my normal daily routine.

He then read on from Maguire's alleged statements. According to these I was alleged in one of them to have lent Maguire a car to blow up B and M Motors in Enniskillen, in another I was alleged to have kept watch for an armed robbery. Maguire was supposed to have me involved exactly the way the "I" statements had earlier. I told them that if they were genuine statements, Maguire was telling lies. They then threatened to bring me face to face with Maguire. I told them to do so. They said that they would, but such a meeting never took place.

I then got another long lecture on how foolish I was and how they were so concerned for my welfare. They went into great detail to explain how I was being given special treatment because of my wife and family and the attitude which I was taking would only lead to me being locked up for a long time in prison. "You don't even care about your wife and seven children," I was told by the Superintendent. "Even if you are released," he continued, "you are now a prime suspect for the UVF and if they don't get you, they'll get some of your children or even your wife or perhaps blow up your home."

He told me that a simple statement from me would take all the attention away from my wife and family. The whole discussion from the previous interview was gone over again. They emphasised their influence over the courts and how they would be able to get me off. They discussed the serious consequences of the two murder statements being produced in court and how my stupidity was giving them no option but to "put me down" for 35 years.

I told them that I was prepared and resigned to go to court and trust in God. I asked them when the court would be and again, I brought up the subject of a solicitor. I told them that I needed one to advise me and to prepare me for court. I went even further by telling my two interviewers that I would not accept their "deal" because in the first place I was not guilty of any terrorist activity and secondly, I could not trust them. If, however, they allowed me to see my solicitor I might perhaps reconsider my decision.

I was told that my court case would possibly be in Enniskillen either on Sunday or more likely on Monday morning. As regards to a solicitor, I was told that solicitors do not get into Castlereagh but that I would be given ample time to consult one before my court case.

After an hour of persuasive and threatening tactics from the two detectives, I still refused to make a statement. Eventually they both packed up their belongings and left the room in disgust. On leaving they both told me that I would regret not cooperating with them because they were sincere and concerned about me and I would realise this when it was too late.

They were immediately replaced by two more detectives. One of these men I knew to be an inspector who had interviewed me on the previous Thursday afternoon. The other man was a tall dark-haired person with a pleasant face. He was about 30 years of age. This interview lasted about two or three hours. At no stage was I abused or threatened in any way. I remained seated throughout. They both had a friendly attitude towards me. We spoke together of politics, education, religion and social work. I pontificated about a united Ireland by peaceful means where both Protestant and Catholic could live together as fellow Irishmen. I condemned the Stormont Government who for 50 years stirred up the Protestant community against the Catholics by gerrymander, victimisation, bigotry in job selection, housing allocation and positioning of factories. I condemned the RUC for allowing themselves to be made tools of this regime and by becoming a political force. Instead of the RUC taking part in civil rights demonstrations they were seen by their actions in Derry and in other centres including Enniskillen as a force of repression against Catholics. I referred to the blatant wall of silence by the RUC after the Samuel Devenney case in Derry. The two detectives were very much in agreement with most of the things I said. I was asked about a speech which I had made during a public meeting in Tempo, which is a small rural town in Co. Fermanagh. They claimed that during my speech I stated, "The only good policeman is a dead one." I explained that I remembered such a thing being said but that I could not remember whether I had said it or not. I went on to say that if I had made that statement, I meant that as a result of the actions of the RUC in trying to suppress the civil rights movement they could not be trusted as being friends of the Catholic people. Therefore, the only kind of policeman one could trust from a Catholic viewpoint was a dead one. This, I explained, did not mean that Catholics were to go out and kill policeman but that they should have as little to do with them as possible. I went on to state that when these kinds of speeches were made in 1968-69 there was no such thing as a policeman being shot or blown up. It was several years before that sort of thing happened. I told them that I fully appreciated the need for a police force but not one which allowed themselves to be the tools of the bigoted Unionist politicians like Bill Craig and Brian Faulkner. The RUC would have a lot to do to become an accepted force to the Catholic community. I said that the only man who had tried to change the RUC was Sir Arthur Young.

The main topic of education which we discussed was the possibility of mixed schools. They were very concerned that both Catholic and Protestant children should attend the same schools. I agreed with this thinking on the subject, but I pointed out that the biggest problem would come from Protestant parents allowing their children to mix with Catholics and not the other way around.

The rest of the morning passed quite quickly. Of course, they eventually got around to asking me to make a statement. I was told that I must make a written confession sooner or later detailing my involvement in terrorist activities. The younger man was very quick to refer to the fact that the previous night I had been willing to make a statement. He told me that I must have something to be guilty about or I would not have considered making a statement. The other man interrupted by telling him that the "deal" was a matter for the two people involved, meaning the Superintendent and his partner.

Eventually a policeman arrived with my dinner. It consisted of minced meat, peas and potatoes. I tried to eat it all because I felt that if I didn't they would accuse me of being so guilty that I couldn't eat. Earlier interrogators had accused me of this. Despite my efforts, I left at least half of it. I was feeling very sick and the sight of food was too much for me. The older man kept smoking his pipe and talking to me during my dinner. He asked me why I wasn't eating and told me that the police get the same dinners as the suspects.

I told him that I could not complain about the quality of the meals but that I was not feeling too good.

He invited me to take a walk with him outside. I was delighted to accept. We both walked up and down the little yard between the interrogation block and the administrative building. I looked longingly up at the high walls which were spiked with glass and topped with barbed wire and wished that I was on the other side of them.

Eventually my companion asked me, "What are you thinking about?"

"I'm very worried about my wife and children," I replied.

"I know the way you feel," he said. "I will do my best to get you back to them. If only you would cooperate with us and tell us all you know I could do a lot for you."

I thanked him for his offer of help in trying to get me released and assured him that I would be deeply indebted to him for anything he would do. I pleaded with him to give up the idea of getting me to sign a statement for something I did not do. He still kept telling me that he was not fully convinced of my innocence but that he had an open mind and would keep in touch with me. He brought me to some outside toilets where I washed my hands and splashed cold water on my face to freshen myself up. I was then brought back to the same interrogation room. After about 10 minutes my interrogators were relieved by two more detectives. One of them had interviewed me the previous Thursday afternoon. The other I recognised as a man who had been a uniformed policeman in Enniskillen some years previously. He was a strong, well-built man, about 5 feet 10 inches in height with a round fat face. He was about 25 years of age. Several times he left the room during this interview in the company of another man from Armagh. Again, this interview was friendly and at no time was I abused or threatened. The interview continued on similar lines to the last one. The man who had interviewed me previously seemed to be acquainting his colleague about my situation by quoting extracts from my file and by his line of questioning. His cross-examination was similar to that of the two previous interviews on Thursday.

I told the other detective that I recognised him. He said that he had known me well in Enniskillen. I then asked him to tell me if he had ever heard of me being involved in terrorism or of even being openly sympathetic towards violence at any time. He said that he knew me to be a very busy man running a driving school after normal teaching hours and also running a youth club. I asked him to convince his colleagues in Castlereagh of this. I told him to read the file and see the things that I was being accused of. While he agreed with me, he said that there must be some small involvement in something to have me there. This always seemed to be the type of conclusion to their interviews. The Armagh detective said that if he had his way, he would release me, but he felt sure that I was going to be charged with something. He said that he was basing this judgement on a conversation he had heard amongst the other detectives. I felt very annoyed by this news.

As the interview went on, another detective came into the room and told me that my doctor had arrived to see me. I could not believe my ears.

15

INTERROGATION 12

Here I must stress the importance of getting a medical examination when offered. It was crucial in my case; I would have been lost without it. I was brought to a waiting room just next to the medical room where I was supervised by a uniformed policeman. He opened a door leading from the waiting room into the medical room and ushered me in. Inside the medical room, which on first impressions seemed to be very elaborately equipped, were two doctors. One, who was sitting on a chair at a table inside the door, was Dr Mulhern, my family doctor from Enniskillen and the other, a small, young, fair-haired man introduced himself as being there to represent the police. I later found out that this man was Dr Dean.

I was delighted to see Dr Mulhern and would have liked to have had a conversation with him and ask him how my family were at home and particularly how my wife was bearing up. However, I felt that such a conversation might only lead to the termination of my medical examination. On seeing Dr Mulhern, I smiled at him and said "Hello." I felt that he was rather shocked at seeing me in the state I was in. He could obviously see that I was unshaven and scruffy looking and I'm quite sure that he could observe the bruise marks to my ears and left eye. After a slight pause he asked me, "Do you wish me to examine you?" I looked at him and said "Yes." I was a little put off by his first words as I felt that it was obvious that I wanted an examination. He even repeated the question and again I said "Yes."

I found it particularly difficult to undress. My whole shoulder and neck muscles seemed to have contracted making it very difficult for me to raise my arms or to move my head from side to side. Although I experienced some degree of pain from such attempted movements the main problem was that I didn't seem to have any power in my arms and shoulders. After several attempts I succeeded in getting my brown woollen jumper off over my head, and although my shirt buttoned up the front I had difficulty in getting my shoulders back far enough to allow the shirt to slide off. I had equal difficulty in removing my now soiled and sweaty vest.

On advice from Dr Dean, the police doctor, my own doctor began to complete the formalities on an official medical form. When he came to the line *I am/I am not alleging assault or ill treatment*, I requested him to state, "I am not alleging assault at this time." Both doctors seemed a little surprised at this request. I then went on to explain that I had been told that an extension order had been granted in my case and that I would probably be held there until the following Wednesday at least. I told them that I feared further ill treatment during the coming days and I felt that they might be easier on me if I didn't wish to complain. I asked Dr Mulhern, at this stage, if he would come back to examine me the following Wednesday so that, if there were any further injuries, he could then submit a complaint to the police authorities. He agreed to do this.

I stood on the floor while Dr Mulhern examined my ears. The other doctor began writing on a form of his own. He sat at the other end of the small room about six feet away from us. Dr Mulhern asked for some items of equipment, such as a stethoscope, as he had not been allowed to bring in his own. He also needed a light to look into my ears. Dr Dean said that he didn't have one with him. Dr Mulhern had to continue the examination without instruments. He examined my ears and head thoroughly. He kept asking me how I had received various bruises. I told him that I had been hit regularly with fists and open hands on my face and head, also on my neck, shoulders, back and stomach. I complained to him about being kicked in the buttocks and legs and of being made to stand in very awkward positions. He asked me to move my head from left to right. I had difficulty in doing this. He wrote down everything he found. I was then asked to remove my trousers and lie down on a medical couch. He examined my chest, on which there was a large bruise mark, my stomach and kidney areas. He pulled down my underpants and examined my private parts. I told him, on being asked, that I had not received any ill treatment in that area. He then examined my legs and feet. At one stage, during this examination, Dr Dean came over to where I was lying to look more clearly at me. He then went back to his end of the room and continued writing.

When Dr Mulhern had ended his examination, I was told to put my clothes back on. This was, I must say, easier said than done. After quite a painful effort I dressed myself. By this time, Dr Mulhern had finished writing his report. Dr Mulhern marked, on the skeleton map provided, the bruise marks which he had found on my body. Dr Dean then advised Dr Mulhern that he should insist on getting his report photocopied. Dr Dean took the report to the uniformed policemen who had remained on duty in the waiting room and asked him to have the photocopy made. A few minutes later the policeman returned with the medical report photocopied. Dr Dean told Dr Mulhern to leave this photocopy with the police in Castlereagh for investigation.

The medical examination lasted 25 to 35 minutes. When it ended, I could not resist asking Dr Mulhern how my wife and children were. He assured me that my wife was in good health and bearing up magnificently under the strain, and that all the children were well. He said that my wife had sent up some underwear and other things and that I would probably get them later. On leaving, I thanked him for his visit and reminded him again of his proposed return on Wednesday. I also asked him not to mention to my wife that I had been ill-treated. I felt that if it became public knowledge that I had been ill-treated in Castlereagh, the result could be that I would be charged with some trumped up offence or other to prevent me relating my experiences.

...ce Station on (date).... 22·1·77 ...... (time)..... 4·15 p.m.

Name..... Bernard O'Connor ..... Address..... Willoughby Close Enniskillen

Date of Birth..... 21·6·42 .

I,..... Bernard O'Connor ..... wish/do-not-wish to be medically examined.
I am not

.... assault or ill-treatment.

Signed..... Bernard O'Connor ..... Witness.....

C/about c/o pain especially around the neck
from being punched. Also c/o epigastric pain from
being punched in stomach.

O/E Marked tenderness over cervical spine with limitation
of flexion and rotation.

Bruise marks to Right and left ears and ....
of left eye. Bruise marks to left anterior chest wall

Marked tenderness on .... palpation

G.U.T. Nil relevant except tenderness in
kidney area.

I agree/do-not-agree to whatever medical treatment may be thought desirable.

Signed..... Bernard O'Connor ..... Signature of Examining MO..... Felix D. Mulhern

Witness..... Date..... Time.....

Status.....

Dr Mulhern's notes during his examination of me in Castlereagh, Saturday 22nd January 1977

I am on the panel of doctors of which the O'Connor family of 38 Willoughby Place are patients. On the evening of Friday the 21 January 1977 at about tea time or shortly after I received a telephone call from Mrs O'Connor in regard to her husband Bernard. I was aware at that time that Bernard O'Connor had been taken in by the police the previous day and was in custody in Belfast. Mrs O'Connor told me that neither a Priest or a solicitor was able to get in to see her husband at Castlereagh where he was detained at Belfast. She asked me would I go down to see her husband as the family doctor would be allowed in to see him. My recollection is that she was making the request for me to go up and not that her husband had asked for a doctor to attend him or that he had asked Mrs O'Connor to have me go and see him. I did not immediately agree to go but asked Mrs O'Connor if she could guarantee that I would be admitted after making the journey to Belfast. She replied that she had already been in touch with the police at Castlereagh and confirmed to me that she had been told that I would be admitted. I have a feeling that she may have rung Castlereagh again to confirm that. I remember I spoke to Mrs O'Connor on the 'phone twice that evening. On the first occasion when Mrs O'Connor rang I did not agree or disagree to go to Belfast but said that I would discuss the matter first with my partner Dr Brennan. I later telephoned Mrs O'Connor and told her that I was prepared to go to Belfast. I told her that I would go up the following afternoon. I think Mrs O'Connor had to let Castlereagh know when to expect me as she asked me what time I would be leaving Enniskillen and I understood that she was therefore going to let Castlereagh know what time I would arrive there. I saw Mrs O'Connor the following day before going to Belfast as I had arranged that she could get someone to drive me to Belfast. I went down to her house and left my car there and was driven to Belfast by a friend of Mrs O'Connor's. She gave me some books and items of clothing for Bernard to deliver to him. The conversation I had with Mrs O'Connor that day prior to going to Belfast was generally about my visit to see Bernard. She made no suggestion to me that he required my assistance medically or did she make any complaint to me that he was being ill treated or anything like that. In fact I looked on the visit more from the welfare

point of view and that I would be able to return to Enniskillen and tell Mrs

O'Connor that her husband was OK. What came across to me was her anxiety over

the fact that only a doctor could get in to see her husband. I am willing to

attend a Police disciplinary hearing for the purpose of giving evidence should

I be required to do so.

                    (Signed) Felix J Mulhern B.A., M.B.

Witness Wm J Davidson   Insp

Certified a true copy of the original _____ Inspector

edical Examination (Initial/Intermediate/Final) at _Castlereagh_

Poli◯ation on (date)... 21/1/77 ... (time)... 4.20 pm

Name... B O'Connor ... Address... Willoughby Place Enniskillen

Date of Birth... 21/6/47

I, ... wish/do not wish to be medically examined.

I am/am not alleging assault or ill-treatment.

Signed.. Witness..

Examination By Dr Mulhern.

State he was beaten & both during interviews

C/o pain Back of head and neck and over Both
clavicles. also C/o generalized pleuretic pain on inspiration
finding bruises over ① post chest

was not examined prior to interviews But states he sustained
bruises during interrogation

C/o pain Both ankles — result of having to stand in
Spread eagled semi flexed position for prolonged periods of time
also tender on palpation — and as result of knees
of punches

made it clear that he was _not_ alleging assault But
wanted the examination as a precaution.

I agree/ do not agree to whatever medical treatment may be thought desirable.

Signed.. Signature of Examining MO... _Dean_

Witness.. Date........................ Time........................

Status..

Report of Dr. Dean who was present during examination by Dr. Mulhern.

STATEMENT OF DR B E DEAN, MEDICAL PRACTITIONER, 281 ORMEAU ROAD,
BELFAST TAKEN BY CHIEF INSPECTOR BROWN AT BELFAST ON 15 MARCH 1977

On the 22nd January 1977 I was called to the Police Office at Castlereagh
to be present during the medical examination of a prisoner by his own
C.P.   I was told on arrival at Castlereagh by the Sergeant that
Bernard O'Connor was the prisoner to be examined and that Dr Mulhern from
Enniskillen was already there to carry out the examination.   I met Dr
Mulhern in the Duty Room of the Police Office.   We introduced each other
and I remember Dr Mulhern saying to me that the family of Mr O'Connor had
contacted him to examine Bernard O'Connor.   I explained to Dr Mulhern my
position in attending the examination on behalf of the Police Authority
and we then went to the Medical Room to await the arrival of Mr O'Connor.
He was brought to us in the Medical Room by a uniformed Constable who then
went outside and closed the door.   Dr Mulhern and I then saw
Bernard O'Connor alone in the Medical Room.   Mr O'Connor recognised
Dr Mulhern and I explained to Mr O'Connor that Dr Mulhern was there at the
request of his family and that I intended to be present during the
examination on behalf of the Police Authority unless he, Mr O'Connor, had
any objection.   Mr O'Connor stated he had no objection to my being present.
I then seated myself on one side of the Medical Room and Mr O'Connor stood
with his back to the desk and Dr Mulhern stood on the opposite side of
Mr O'Connor from me.   I was looking at Mr O'Connor's right profile and
Dr Mulhern at his left.   Dr Mulhern asked Mr O'Connor did he want him,
Dr Mulhern, to examine him, and Mr O'Connor replied that he did.   Dr Mulhern
then asked Mr O'Connor if he had any aches or pains or something to that
effect to initiate the history.   I'm not sure of the precise words.
Mr O'Connor complained of pain to the back of his head and neck and over both
clavicles.   Dr Mulhern asked him what caused this pain and Mr O'Connor
replied that it was because he had been beaten with fists during interviews.

Mr O'Connor also complained of generalized pleuritic pain on inspiration.

Mr Mulhern then asked him to strip to his underpants. The doctor then commenced a detailed examination of Mr O'Connor. He looked through his hair for any sign of bruising on scalp but did not remark on seeing any bruising or any bumps. I remember him remarking that he did not see any. He then examined Mr O'Connor's ears and asked Mr O'Connor to point out any place where he felt discomfort. I remember Mr O'Connor fingering at his ears but I cannot remember if it was one ear or both or what ear it was if only one. Dr Mulhern looked closely at Mr O'Connor's ears and also at his head and face. He was only a matter of inches from Mr O'Connor while looking at his head and ears. I remained seated about 4 to 5 feet from Mr O'Connor but had an opportunity to see Mr O'Connor's head both right and left as Dr Mulhern asked him to rotate for the examination although I had only fleeting glances of his left profile and had the greater opportunity to see his right profile. Dr Mulhern did not move from his position on the opposite side to Mr O'Connor and did not block my view of Mr O'Connor at any time during the examination. I saw no evidence of bruising on Mr O'Connor's head, neck or ears. If Dr Mulhern suggests that there was bruising to the right and left ears and to the corner of the left eye, certainly I was not aware of any from my position. It is possible that there might have been faint or fading bruising which Dr Mulhern could have seen when only inches away from Mr O'Connor. When Dr Mulhern examined Mr O'Connor's neck he asked him to flex his neck so that his chin touched the sternum and then to extend his head to the limit. He then asked Mr O'Connor to rotate his head to right and left as far as possible. Mr O'Connor complained of pain at the back of his neck at the extremities of each movement but his neck movements appeared full. On palpation of the cervical vertabrae Mr O'Connor experienced some degree of pain. Dr Mulhern examined both clavicles but there did not appear to be any local tenderness. Dr Mulhern then examined the chest wall particularly in the area of the left pectoralis rigor. This was the area Mr O'Connor described the pleuritic pain, and it was in this area that there was visible bruising. From where I sat the bruising appeared to be greenish black in colour and about 4 to 5 inches in diameter with ill defined margins. It is difficult to define the time at which such a bruise was caused as it depends on a number of factors including the strength of the blow and whether an instrument was used and the area of the body involved. In my opinion and from my observation of the bruise I consider that it had been caused some one to three days previously. It is possible that the injuries described could have been caused as Mr O'Connor describes but it is also possible that they could have been self inflicted. The underpants that Mr O'Connor was wearing were of the white Y-front variety and gave a clear view to the groins. Although Mr O'Connor complained of pain in both calves I could see no external evidence of any injury. He complained of pain in the calves as the result of having to stand in a spreadeagled semi-flexed position for prolonged periods of time. I do not recall Mr O'Connor's underpants being pulled down during Dr Mulhern's examination to give a view of the buttocks. Dr Mulhern then asked Mr O'Connor to lie on the examination couch. He auscultated the heart area and the lungs front and back. He paid particular attention to the left anterior chestwall ie the bruised area but the air entry appeared normal and he did not mention any added sounds. He then palpated the abdomen and Mr O'Connor experienced pain in the epigastric area. I heard him also complain of pain in the lower abdomen but in this area Dr Mulhern did not appear to elicit tenderness. From my position I could not discern any bruising over the abdominal wall. When in the sitting position on the couch Dr Mulhern elicited tenderness in the kidney area . At that stage the examination concluded and Dr Mulhern told Mr O'Connor he could get dressed again. While Mr O'Connor was getting dressed Dr Mulhern sat down at the desk to write his report. I explained to Dr Mulhern that when a GP is called in he normally writes his report in the sort of form that is on the desk, which is especially designed for this purpose as it has a diagram on the back to show location of bruises or other injury. Dr Mulhern

....e his report on one of the medical forms which are numbered 39/17(b).
After Mr O'Connor was clothed again Dr Mulhern put the question to him
whether he was alleging assault.   When he was asked this Mr O'Connor
hesitated and then despite having been subjected to the extensive medical
examination stated that he did not wish to allege ill-treatment.   This
appeared incongruous to Dr Mulhern and myself but Mr O'Connor inferred that
the reason for this was that he feared further ill-treatment at the hands
of the police after we had gone.   This after all was not a final examination.
The lighting in the medical room where this examination was carried out is
good and is derived from both artifical light and natural light from a
window.   The examination lasted approximately 25 minutes and from my
observations there did not appear any medical reason why Mr O'Connor was not
fit for further detention and at no time did Mr O'Connor intimate that he
wanted released on medical grounds.   During Dr Mulhern's examination Mr
O'Connor did not appear to be anxious or agitated.   He showed no sign of
physical or mental stress and his general appearance was normal for his
situation.   During the examination I recorded Dr Mulhern's findings but
did not enter into a discussion about them.   I have seen the medical report
prepared by myself on Form 39/17(b) concerning my observations when present
with Dr Mulhern.   The date at the top is incorrect and should read the
22 January 1977.

                    (Signed)   B Dean
                           MB EM PAO DCH DRCOG

Certified a true copy of the original _____. Inspector

16

BACK IN ENNISKILLEN
22ND JANUARY

Meanwhile, back in Enniskillen, my wife Patricia was bearing up magnificently under the strain. Here she tells how she spent Saturday, 22nd January.

On Saturday morning, I phoned Castlereagh and was told that there was no change. I told the RUC man to whom I was speaking that Dr Mulhern would be leaving Enniskillen at around one o'clock and if Barney was getting home would he let me know so that the doctor would not be making such a long journey for nothing. He assured me that he would.

When Dr Mulhern arrived at the house before he left Enniskillen, I checked again with Castlereagh just to be sure. I gave the doctor a few things for Barney and asked him to tell him that the RUC had taken a record, a blank tape and words of two songs. Eamonn Cox, who had agreed to drive the doctor to Belfast, had arrived earlier and they both left around one o'clock.

I felt a little better then with the thought that someone would get in to see Barney. I was also kept busy answering the phone and with callers, as I had been on Thursday and Friday. At that time, Barney was running a driving school, but as I had just had the baby, there were very few lessons booked and his partner, Hugh Ward, was able to cope with those we could not cancel.

It was around teatime when Dr Mulhern and Eamonn arrived back. Everyone in the house seemed to disappear and I was left on my own with the doctor in the living room. I asked him how Barney was and he answered, "Mentally, he's very alert." I repeated the question and got the same answer. I then asked, "How does he look?" Dr Mulhern then told me that Barney had been abused physically. I kept saying, "My God, my God." I then asked how badly Barney had been abused and Dr Mulhern told me that it was bad enough, but that he had no abrasions or broken bones and was in good spirits. I asked him if Barney had made a complaint and Dr Mulhern told me that he had said, "No, not at this time," but that he had asked the doctor to go back to visit him again on Wednesday. The doctor said that he had agreed to do this. He then told me that Barney had asked him not to tell anyone at home that he had been abused. But he felt that as I had been the one who had asked him to go, he was willing to tell me.

After Dr Mulhern left, I told everyone in the house that the doctor had found Barney in good spirits and that he was going back to see him on Wednesday. I then drove Eamonn to his home and, on the way, I confided in him about what the doctor had told me. When I arrived home, I heard that two of the others who had been arrested were on their way home and that a third was being charged at a special court in Enniskillen on Sunday morning. I was now convinced that I would not see Barney until Wednesday at the earliest. I kept trying to figure out why the RUC had arrested him in the first place and why they had abused him. Slowly the penny dropped and all the things I had read about Castlereagh Holding Centre and Fr Fall and Fr Murray's condemnation of it. I felt ashamed that I had read of these things happening, but as I was not personally involved it just had not sunk in. I wondered how many other good Christians like myself there were who shrugged off those things as being no concern of theirs. It is easy to sit back and pretend that it doesn't happen. And if it does, it's only to a few who had been arrested with weapons or bombs in their possessions. I realise now how foolish I was.

As on the previous two days, Frank and Mrs Maguire phoned every hour. I didn't tell them that Barney had been abused, as I was by this time suspicious that the phone was being tapped. I was afraid that if I was overheard, Barney might get twice as much.

Before going to bed that Saturday night, I phoned Castlereagh and spoke to the desk sergeant. He said that he was just doing relief and did not know how Bernard

O'Connor was. He thought that there was no one in the cells. When I mentioned Enniskillen, he said that there was a young man from there who was waiting for transport home. But after a few minutes said that it was not Barney. I discovered afterwards that in fact Barney was not in the cell at that time but that he was in the interrogation block.

When Fr Mullan called, I told him of the abuse. It was impossible to get to sleep on Saturday night as I kept wondering if the abuse was still going on.

17

INTERROGATION 15

When I got back to my cell, I spent a long time thinking over methods of interrogation which were used by the two detectives. Although I was at this stage physically very weak, my mind was extremely active. I lay on the top of the bed looking up at the ceiling and thought and thought. I could not sleep even though I made a conscious effort to do so; I could not relax or get my mind to stop turning over the turmoil of the past three days.

I came to the conclusion that the idea behind the interview methods used by the last two interrogators was to leave me mentally exhausted to such an extent that I could not concentrate on what I was saying. As a result, I would answer the questions on terrorist activities the way they wanted me to, and I would sign statements incriminating myself in serious crimes, which I had nothing to do with.

I tried to say the Rosary in thanksgiving to God for being able to withstand the pressure put on me by both the detectives. I emphasise the fact that I tried to say a Rosary because I could not concentrate on any one subject for more than a few seconds at a time. I was going from one thought to another despite my earnest efforts to concentrate on the Rosary. To say any more than two or three Hail Marys in a row was now impossible, the result being that I began each decade numerous times and must have said the Hail Mary 15 or 20 times for each decade.

My entire concept of time seems to have gone astray at this stage. I felt that I had remained in my cell until after lunch on Sunday, yet the police files had records shown that I was interrogated again from ten o'clock on Sunday morning. I remember, however, each person who interviewed me on Sunday and the form each of them took. But as to the timing of such interviews, I could only be giving my opinion. To help me with this problem, I have been furnished by the police with the times and durations of all interviews while in Castlereagh. Although the times given by the police and those estimated by me differ, I have no reason to doubt that these, given by the RUC for Sunday, are correct. For example, I did not think that I was interviewed by the detectives on Sunday until about two or three in the afternoon, yet the police state that I was interviewed by detectives from ten o'clock that morning. However, I do remember clearly being interviewed by those two men.

Before I go on to relate what happened during my interviews on Sunday, I will relate the events which took place in my cell that morning. I was served with the now familiar sausage, egg and soda bread for breakfast. Despite my efforts to force myself to eat it, I was unable to consume very much. I tried washing it down with large mouthfuls of tea, but it was to no avail. I just kept getting sick with every bit of food I tried to put in my mouth. After breakfast, when the policeman came to take away the remainder of the meal, I asked his permission to get a drink of water. He allowed me to bring a beaker of water back to my cell so that I could have a drink whenever I felt thirsty. He also gave me two of my Penbritin tablets.

I sat on the chair in the corner of the cell. I began thinking of the whole terrible business over and over again. Suddenly a thought struck me. It was Sunday and I had no opportunity of going to Mass. I would not claim to be an outstanding member of the Catholic Church, but there is one thing I have always felt proud of and that is that I had never missed Mass on a Sunday. I felt so annoyed at the idea of missing Mass that Sunday so I decided to say it for myself. That was the extent of how far my brain had been taxed mentally.

I proceeded to go through the form of Mass myself. I used the chair as an altar and the beaker of water as my chalice with a sugar cube, which I had kept from my breakfast, as the host. Owing to my inability to concentrate for any length of time it must have taken me about an hour to get through the liturgy. I had little difficulty remembering the prayers and responses at the beginning of Mass simply because I had been saying them every Sunday for the previous 30 years anyway. It was no great strain on my brain to remember them, but the problem lay in concentrating long enough to be able to finish a prayer. The scripture readings, however, presented problems. The only extracts from the Bible which came clearly to my mind were the passion and death of our Lord on the cross. I imagined that I was reading the story of the agony of our Lord in the garden and carrying the cross to Mount Calvary. I eventually got through the readings despite my mind wandering on numerous occasions. At the consecration I held up the sugar cube and the beaker of water in turn, just as the priest does with the bread and wine at Mass. I felt really delighted at having succeeded in getting through the ceremony. It seemed to have given me feelings of strength and satisfaction.

I imagined that the entire morning had been used up while thinking and saying Mass. Apart from the time spent saying Mass, I found it hard to adjust to being on my own. I was now so used to talking that I wanted someone to talk to. I was conditioned to being interrogated.

A strange thing happened during my time alone, that Sunday morning. I went to the toilet to get a drink and during the few minutes I was absent from my cell someone left a religious tract on my bed. I remember reading it on my return and the whole message of the tract was that the sinner must repent. I also had two small red packets of Tate and Lyle sugar cubes under my pillow and these were missing when I returned from the toilet.

The Sunday interview began with a pleasant looking detective. He gave me the impression that he was a very religious man who was well versed on sacred scripture. Several times during the interview, he quoted long passages of scripture to me. He spent a long time on examples from the Bible in which sinners were forgiven. All the time he spoke in a calm, pleasant and mellow-toned voice. He told me that it was obvious from talking to me and even looking at me that I was a good Christian who had allowed myself to be led into temptation in the form of terrorism. He said that God, knowing this, was beaming down from heaven at me, waiting for me to repent. He elaborated on how lucky I was to be given such a chance by God. He quoted examples of Provos who were killed on bombing and shooting missions without having the chance to repent. He emphasised the point that several policemen and soldiers had not been given such a chance to prepare themselves to meet their God before being shot by Provos like me. He told me not to turn my back on God because he might never give me another chance to repent. I kept trying to convince him that God was perfectly happy with me because I had nothing on my conscience to repent about. However, all my protestations of innocence were in vain. He just kept on preaching to me.

To prove his sincerity, he told me of a teenage girl from the Falls Road in Belfast who had got herself involved in terrorism with the Provos. He had interviewed the girl and her widowed mother after she had been caught by the police. He produced a letter from his inside pocket written on blue paper. He folded down the address at the top of the page telling me at the same time that he could not let me see it due to security reasons. He then read the letter to me. It was allegedly from the girl's mother. Her daughter had been sentenced to six years imprisonment and she was thanking this detective for getting the girl the prison sentence to keep her safe from the Provos and acts of terrorism. It went on to state that the mother was glad to have her girl in prison because she was now safe and would be a far better person when released. He showed me the handwriting, but I was unable to see either the address at the top or the signature at the bottom of the letter.

During the interview, another detective whom I had met the previous day, came into the room. He did not really take much of a part in interviewing me but acted more or less as a backup to the other one. Eventually, a third detective came into the room. He did not tell us his name, but according to police files, I was able to find his name. He was a tall, well-built man of about 35 years of age and had fair hair. The first two detectives then left the room, taking with them a small handgun, which the religious man had produced from his pocket of his navy jacket and given to the other detective who was staying.

This detective did not have either the personality or the diplomacy of the other two detectives. He had a very gruff attitude and told me that I was a guilty Provo and it was bloody well time that I caught myself on and confessed to the crimes I had committed. He accused me over and over again of all the things that had been thrown at me for the previous three days. He told me that there was not any doubt about my guilt and that sooner or later I was going to confess. He said that holding out was not going to save me. He then told me that I must be a nobody about Enniskillen because no other person other than my wife had bothered to contact them or bothered to phone about me. He went on to try and demoralise me by trying to convince me that despite all my efforts to run the Boy Scouts, the community centre or the civil rights movement in Enniskillen, nobody gave a damn about me. Finally, the religious detective arrived back and continued to try to persuade me to write a confession to all of the crimes he claimed I had committed. Eventually, much to his apparent disgust, he claimed that I had flown in the face of God and rejected a chance to show sorrow for all my alleged crimes. He must have spent almost an hour trying to convince me, "For God's sake, repent." At last, he brought me back to my cell.

18

INTERROGATION 16

Although I cannot record exactly the sequence of events during Sunday, I do recollect the various incidents which took place, especially that afternoon. Lunch, the usual fry-up, was served to my cell and I was also given my quota of Penbritin tablets around midday. I am not able to be specific about the amount of food which I ate, but I am correct in stating that the longer I stayed in Castlereagh, the harder it became to force myself to eat. I attempted, during lapses of concentration, to say my Rosary of thanksgiving and my Rosary of preparation between interrogation sessions. I can safely say that prayers kept me sane and able to fight on.

I was brought for interrogation that Sunday afternoon by a detective I had not seen before. I noted that he was rather slovenly dressed in comparison to all the other men who had interviewed me up to this point. He wore grey flannels and a polo neck jumper. When we reached the interrogation block, none of the interview rooms were open. Another detective came along the corridor and he offered to go back to get a key to one of the rooms. My new interrogator and I stood facing each other with our backs to the doors, which were opposite. During the few minutes in which we were standing there, he told me that he was very surprised at a Catholic school teacher being so deeply involved in violence. He went on to say that I was a disgrace to my religion and totally unfit to be the father of seven children. I was, he stated, a person who was unable to hold my position of responsibility in life. He said that locking me up would be too good for me. His sharp brown beady eyes, set in fat chubby cheeks, stared fixedly on me while he spoke. I did not even attempt to reply. I had grown so used to comments like these during interrogations that I did not see any point in wasting time trying to convince him of the truth.

When the other man returned with the key to the door of room five, I entered with the two detectives. The second one who had fetched the key was a man whom I had met before. He was the small, fat, blonde detective who had offered me a drink of Lucozade, only to snatch it away again during the first night in Castlereagh, when I had been severely beaten until about three o'clock in the morning. The other new detective expressed disgust with me for being such a vicious terrorist.

During this interview, neither of the two men attempted to abuse me physically. The blonde detective's attitude towards me was completely opposite to that of the Thursday night/early Friday morning episode. He spent his time flicking through my file and asking me over and over again to make a confession to the alleged offences which were mentioned in it. He stressed the point that lying my way out of Castlereagh was not going to save me because the UVF were only willing and waiting for the chance to shoot me. He emphasised the theory that I would be better alive in prison and doing time for my crimes than lying dead. Either way, he told me he didn't care. The problem lay in my hands and he hoped that I would have sense.

The other man had a different style of interviewing me. His legs straddled each side of the chair, which was facing backwards. He leaned forward with his arms folded over the back of the chair, and his chin resting on his hands. He kept looking straight into my eyes. He went on about my standing in the community as a teacher and leader and pillar of the church. He also reminded me of my involvement with the People's Democracy and the civil rights campaign. He said that I was a total failure and a let-down to everyone in Enniskillen. He claimed I was a bigoted Catholic who had resorted to the IRA to further my bigotry.

He told me that he had been raised in a Catholic area. His mother and father used to bring him to church every Sunday and they were made join in family prayer at home. He went on to boast that when he reached the age of 16, he left home, matured and learnt to have a mind of his own. He said that he had stopped going to church at that age and was no longer under the thumb of anyone with a dog collar. He concluded his long attack on the Catholic Church by saying, "If there was less religion in the north and more Christianity, then there would be less fighting."

In the middle of this interview, after his long lecture on religion, he began interrogating me again about my alleged acts of terrorism. He took the file in his hand and said in a sarcastic way, "We are investigating the activities of a man called Bernard O'Connor. Do you know anyone of that name?"

"Yes," I answered.

"This Bernard O'Connor happens to live in Enniskillen. Do you know of a Bernard O'Connor living in Enniskillen?"

"Yes," I answered again.

"Well, this Bernard O'Connor mentioned in this file happens to live at 38 Willoughby Place in Enniskillen. Do you know him?"

"I live at 38 Willoughby Place, Enniskillen and my name is Bernard O'Connor, but I have never met the Bernard O'Connor you are talking about."

My interrogator seemed to be enraged by my reply. He banged the table in front of him and shouted at me.

"Who the f*** do you think you are? The Christ?"

At that precise moment and before another word could be spoken, someone walked past the cellblock outside the interrogation room. He was whistling the tune 'Jesus Christ Superstar'.

I was immediately influenced by this. I felt that it was too amazing to be a coincidence. I took it then to be a sign from God to keep up my struggle against the pressure I was under.

Neither he nor I showed any signs of reaction to the whistling. I talked to myself mentally without showing any outward signs of doing so. The detective kept on talking. He was now becoming rather aggressive towards me. He accused me of being the real guilty Bernard O'Connor and said I deserved all that was coming to him. He continued to try to convince me that I was going to get a life sentence in the court. He said that he had no sympathy for me, even though I was going to be locked up away from my wife and seven children for a long time. He advised me to cut out the messing and be honest with myself. He said that I would crack sooner or later. So therefore, why prolong the agony? Several times one of them would read extracts from my file and then look at me in a sarcastic grinning way and say: "O'Connor, you have been the right bastard. Thanks be to God, your game is up."

They would then elaborate on my alleged activities which to them merited bestowing the title "bastard" on me. They praised their so-called informant who had the courage to give the information about me. They told me that this person had been so sickened by my activities and the fact that I was leading the young people of Enniskillen astray by involving them in terrorism, that his conscience had pricked him so hard, that he decided to save the town and the innocent people of Enniskillen by reporting me.

I told him that if anyone was using me in this way, they were doing so to either let themselves or someone else off the hook. I went on to say that I would be the ideal person for anyone to use as a scapegoat so that the police would be side-tracked away from the real "godfather" who was responsible for all the acts of violence in Enniskillen. I asked for the name of the informant, whom I believed was probably sitting back laughing at the idea of me being arrested. However, I did not impress the interrogators with this line of thought. The blonde fellow continued to insist that I was the right man and that I was not going to be able to fool him or anyone else in Castlereagh. Eventually, I was brought back to my cell. Earlier that afternoon when I was being taken for interrogation, the uniformed policeman who was escorting me had difficulty opening the door. On my arrival back to the cell, the policeman could not get the key to turn in the door and he told me that I would have to go to the next cell. This door was closed behind me and the key turned in the lock.

19

INTERROGATION 17

Cell nine was similar to the previous cell. The paintwork was a greyish colour like before and the sizes of the furnishings were exactly the same. The only difference was that the walls in cell number nine displayed a lot of people's initials and dates. I remember thinking at the time that I would remember as many as I could, but alas I know I cannot guess even one of the initials.

My tea that Sunday evening consisted of the now regular greasy fry, more sausages, beans and chips. After nearly four days in the place, one could have thought that food would be welcomed, but the opposite proved to be the case. The very sight of food was enough to make me feel sick. Eventually I felt that I should try and eat as much as I could. But the actual physical act of eating was beyond me. I tried to wash some down with several mouthfuls of tea as I had done many times before, but I had to give up the attempt with about three quarters of the meal remaining. I must state, however, that I am not criticising the standard of the meals, but pointing out my personal condition and the difficulty I had in forcing myself to eat.

Prayer was one of the main factors in keeping me sane. I continued to struggle through my usual Rosary. However, despite many attempts to persevere with the decades and the Mysteries, I eventually managed to get to the end. I would estimate, without exaggeration, that at times I had said between 20 and 30 Hail Marys per decade instead of 10.

The expected but always dreaded ritual of bolts banging and keys turning, followed by the steady thud of boots leading to the cell door, began again. I was once more called for interview. On reaching the table at the entrance hall, I recognised the detective standing there as the one who had interviewed me on Friday. He was bending down, signing the sheets for my release for interview. I was frightened to see that it was him again. I dreaded another interrogation session similar to the one that he and his friend had put me through the previous Friday morning.

The detective walked in front of me down the five steel steps leading from the cellblock. I staggered along slowly behind him. My legs were in such a terrible state of pain that I could scarcely bear to bend them to walk. The muscles right up from the backs of my legs into my thighs had tightened, leaving me in extreme pain when I tried to walk.

Having reached the bottom steps long before me, the detective asked me why I was walking so slowly. I, feeling that he would get some element of delight and satisfaction from my suffering, said that I was finding it difficult to walk in shoes without laces. Walking across the yard to the interrogation block, he again asked if there was something wrong with me. I then told him that my legs were very sore, and he asked me how that had happened. I replied that I had been made to stand in a very awkward manner for a considerable length of time, and that my legs had also been kicked during interview. He did not pursue the subject any further.

On arriving at interrogation room five, I recognised a second detective as the one who had also interrogated me in an extremely cruel manner the previous Friday morning when I had been heavily punched about the head and stomach. I wondered if this interrogation was going to be the same. The smaller of the two men began by explaining that I was the cause of him having to leave his visitors at home to come to interview me. He said that he had not seen these friends for a long time and if I had made a confession the previous day, he could have been free to entertain them. I told him that I was not going to make a confession to something I had no act or part in, but that I was sorry that I was the cause of him not being able to remain with his visitors. Neither of them was willing to accept my claims of innocence. They began to question me again as all the other interrogators had done, about the same terrorist activities in Enniskillen. It went on and on.

Eventually they began to talk about my opinion of the civil rights movement and queried my politics. I went into detail of how I believed that there should be a united Ireland where both Protestants and Catholics would live together in peace and harmony. I said that there would be no peace in Ireland until Britain withdrew from the six counties and took with her all the guns she had put into the province. I pointed out that the disarming and disbanding of the UDR would be a major step forward in winning the confidence and support of the Catholic community. I praised the work done by Sir Arthur Young while he was head of the RUC and I said that he had tried to remove guns from the Northern Ireland situation by disarming the police. The taller detective became very annoyed by this and he began to bang his fist on the table. In a very bigoted outburst, he shouted, "It will be over my dead body that a tricolour will fly over the city hall in Belfast!" I reasoned with him that such an outburst only proved that he had a very sectarian upbringing. I argued that the colours of the flag over the city hall did not matter one bit. It was the unification of the ordinary working people like him and me, to make the island of Ireland a better place to live in and work in, that really mattered. I proposed that it might be a good idea to have no flags and have a united people working for the ideal rather than fighting over a piece of cloth.

The civil rights organisation came under attack from both men. They could see nothing but evil in the motives and objectives of the NICRA. Again, I defended my beliefs in this organisation but despite my efforts to explain the necessity for such a movement and its successes, I was not doing much of a job in convincing them to the civil rights cause. Instead, I suffered another insulting attack from them both, from the taller one in particular. He demanded that I give reasons for my involvement in civil rights. I was told by him that I didn't lack any rights as I had been educated free, had my teacher training free and was now in a good job drawing a steady salary from the state. He even pointed out that I had been able to buy my own house and car. I said that in fact my parents had paid for my grammar school education for three years and that really all this business of "free this and free that" was only a myth, because with the payments of income tax, superannuation and National Insurance contributions from one's salary, there is nothing really free.

I went on to explain that I was concerned about the conditions of others here in Fermanagh and I was laughed at. They thought it was a great joke to hear that more than 60% of the rural houses in Fermanagh had no running water or toilet facilities. I was told that it was none of my business when I informed them that only two of 72 school bus drivers were Catholics in 1969. They could not accept that there was discrimination in employment in the civil service, library service and the hospital authorities. They argued that the fact that there was not one Catholic ambulance driver in

Fermanagh in 1969 was not discrimination. I was accused of being a Catholic bigot for pointing these things out to them.

Despite my many examples of discrimination, gerrymandering and denial of basic civil rights in Fermanagh, my two interrogators remained as unconvinced at the end of my account as they were at the beginning. I told them that I had a right to fight for civil rights as I did not want my children to be brought up in a society of bigotry and hatred. I told him that if people like themselves would only think for a while and forget about the "flag waving, no surrender" type of gutter politics and help to change society, then we would all be playing a part in making this country a wonderful place to live in.

I feel that if I had attempted to carry out such a conversation with the same pair of detectives on the previous Friday morning, I would have received a beating for my efforts. However, even though they were aggressive in their defence of their bigoted principles, they did not at any time give me the impression that they were going to abuse me in any way. Neither did they show me any more photographs of mutilated bodies, which, incidentally, is in breach of their rights as interrogators. Eventually, at the end of two or three hours of continuous conversation, they resorted back to trying to encourage me to sign statements for them. A remarkable fact struck me at this stage. When I stressed the point to them quite clearly that I was innocent of having been involved with terrorist activities or of having any knowledge of such activities, they did not continue to insist otherwise, as had been done previously. Instead, they just closed the file after replacing the notes and I was politely brought back to my cell. I had the impression that perhaps they were beginning to realise my innocence.

It was after this interview that a young, uniformed policeman came to my cell and asked if I would like to have a shower. I was very glad of this offer as there was a heavy smell of sweat coming from my clothes and feet. I had been without a shave for five days and had a beard which was now growing and causing a great irritation to my face and neck. I told the policeman that I would love a shower and a shave, and he explained that he could get me a towel and soap but he doubted if he could get a razor. He said that he would have loaned me a razor himself, but he did not live in Castlereagh police station. He said he could try to get one from one of the other policemen. He returned after about 20 minutes with soap and a towel, but he had been unable to obtain a razor. He then led me to the washing and toilet area at the end of the block and pointed out the shower cubicle. At this stage he explained that, owing to work developments being carried out in Castlereagh, the heating system was out of order and the only shower available was a cold one. I was not unduly worried by this at the time, for the cell block was very hot and stuffy. However, when he turned on the tap the gush of freezing cold water hitting my sweaty body stunned me breathlessly. I had forgotten that it was the middle of a freezing cold winter but the water soon refreshed my memory never mind my body. On reflection I could not understand how the heating system was working so well yet there was no hot water for a shower?

Sunday night and interrogations being over, I was now back in my cell for the rest of the night. I was finding it hard to understand what was going on during the different interrogations. By now, none of the interrogators were even threatening violence, let alone using it, nor were they as persistent in their questioning as the handsome, religious, gospel-persuading detective or the staunch Unionist bigot who had returned me to my cell after the last aggressive interrogation. There seemed to be less of a commitment on their part to prove me guilty. When I stressed my innocence, they no longer persisted with demands for statements or signing confessions. Instead, they were now changing the subject to politics, education and even sport.

I had a visitor to my cell that night and he helped to lighten my burden. He was a small, stout, dark featured, uniformed policeman who was on duty in the cellblock where I was being detained. He was about 50 years of age and spoke with a soft Derry or North Tyrone accent. He told me that he found the place very lonely and quiet, and did I mind if he came into my cell for a chat? He asked where I was from and how long I had been detained. He seemed very sympathetic towards me and expressed the belief that I would be soon released. He showed concern when I told him that I had a rough time with some of the interrogators. He told me that he never got a chance to know what was going on in Castlereagh as he was seldom picked to do duty there. He only did duty in Castlereagh on a relief basis if a man became ill or went off on leave.

He then told me all about himself. He related many stories of his years as a constable in Strabane on the Donegal Tyrone border. He did not like Belfast and longed for the day when he would return to Tyrone and especially Strabane. He said that he had never prosecuted anyone, but rather would persuade people to keep within the law. For example, if he met a young fella driving a car without tax, he would follow him and tell him to get his car taxed, or else he would summons him the next time. He felt that such people would get their car taxed without having to be prosecuted. He gave other examples of this policy which included tipping off publicans in Strabane in advance of planned police raids to catch them serving drink after hours.

Eventually he asked me if I would like a cup of coffee and a sandwich. I was delighted to accept. He went off down the corridor and returned with his flask of coffee and a plastic lunch box. For a change I enjoyed a couple of his beef sandwiches and a beaker of warm coffee without getting sick. He rambled on for hours about life in Strabane and especially about his smuggling escapades across the river that flows along the border between County Donegal and County Tyrone. When he discovered that I was interested in music and enjoyed playing Irish traditional music he was in his element. He loved country and western music, his favourite group being Brian Coll and the Buckaroos. This was a coincidence for I enjoyed this group as well and I particularly admired the singing qualities of Brian Coll. My uniformed friend knew members of the group personally and we had a long discussion about them. He talked for hours. He was obviously feeling a lot more tired than I was, judging by the number of yawns he gave. He decided to move out and lock the door for the night, taking his flask and lunch box with him. Before he left, I expressed my pleasure in his company and thanked him particularly for the coffee and the sandwiches.

20

BACK IN ENNISKILLEN
23RD JANUARY

Sunday was also an eventful day for my wife at home in Enniskillen. The following are the details of her day as told by her.

On Sunday morning I phoned Castlereagh and was told, "Still no change." I was assured that Barney had got the parcel I had sent with Dr Mulhern. After lunch I again phoned Castlereagh and asked the desk sergeant to inquire if Barney needed anything. He left the phone and on returning he informed me that Barney needed a complete change of clothing. I told him that I had sent a change of clothes in Saturday's parcel. I then asked if I would be granted a visit to my husband. I was told that such a request would have to be put to the CID in Enniskillen. I immediately phoned the Enniskillen CID and was informed that it was up to the Chief Inspector to grant me a visit, but that he was not available at the moment. The officer I was speaking to seemed to know me and said that as soon as he could contact the CI, he would phone me back. The CI himself rang me about an hour later and I put my request to him. He assured me that it was not in his power and that this was a case of "passing the buck." He continued to tell me that the arrests in Enniskillen had nothing to do with him and that he had not even known about this until the early hours of Thursday morning, when he was called out of his bed to organise the arrests of five people on the request of the Special Squad from Belfast. I asked him what the police in Belfast would have known about Barney, and that he himself must know that Barney was not in any way involved in crimes. The CI agreed and told me not to worry, as Barney would probably be home soon and that he himself would know who had been the cause of him being arrested.

I then phoned Mrs Maguire, the MP's wife, and told her what had taken place as regards my request for a visit. I also phoned my solicitor and he told me that he had rung Castlereagh and asked for his calls to be recorded. He had also asked for a visit and had been refused permission. As usual, I kept ringing Castlereagh about every hour. The answer was always the same: still no change and no word of release. On Sunday night, our oldest son, Phillip, took a severe pain in the stomach with vomiting and high temperature. I spent the night trying to keep him cool with cold drinks and regular sponging. It was a night of no sleep and worry for me.

21

INTERROGATION 18 AND 19

My memory of time on Monday was just as hazy as it had been the day before, although I am quite clear in my mind as to the sequence of interviews, the interrogators and other events of that day. After the first two or three days in Castlereagh, one's mind becomes disorientated, especially in matters of time. Firstly, as there is no clock on any of the walls in either the detention block or the interview block, a detainee cannot see the time. Secondly, as there is no natural light in the cell, one has no way of knowing whether it is day or night. Although meals were served at set times, my experience showed that interviews were not generally interrupted to serve meals at these times, with the result that it was impossible to guess the time in relation to the meals.

My first interview on Monday was rather strange. I estimated the time to be around 10 a.m., but police records show it to have begun shortly before 3 p.m. I estimated that the duration of this interview was at least an hour, but records again show that it lasted for less than half an hour. I am in no position to be able to dispute the police records of the times involved as I had not at any time seen a watch or clock before 9 that night. I now realise that my brain was too muddled to be able to recollect any detail.

The shortness of this interview was one of the surprising aspects of it, but the two interrogators involved amazed me even more. They were the same two men who had tortured me so severely on my first night in Castlereagh. When I was taken from my cell by the uniformed policemen, I was not prepared to see who was standing at the table waiting to sign me out. For there in his neat stylish suit was the more refined of the two interrogators. I felt very sick at the sight of him. I was dreading the thought of another interview with him. He ushered me out of the cellblock in front of him. I walked slowly but did not talk to him. He took me to room two and there waiting for us was the other more crude and tough interrogator who had abused me so much during their last interview with me. I kept praying to myself for I was scared and felt that this would be "it." Here I was back in the same room with the two men who had almost killed me before.

"Take a seat," I was told by one of them. I got such a shock from hearing these words that I cannot remember who said them. My two interviewers sat on the other side of the table. The now familiar file was planted in front of them. It was by now at least an inch and a half thick. Both men read from it at regular intervals. They talked to me in a normal manner without being over friendly. They told me that they were surprised to see that I had still not made a statement confessing to some terrorist crime or other. They did not accept my pleas of innocence. They spent most of the interview giving me advice; advice which I had heard so often at this stage. I was told that to leave Castlereagh without making a confession would be like committing suicide. I would not stand a chance outside because the UVF would get me within six months. They painted a pitiful picture of my wife and seven children facing the future without a father in the home. They told me that it was my duty as a responsible father to keep myself alive. They encouraged me again and again to sign a statement which would get me into prison and get a sentence which would keep me safe from the Protestant paramilitaries. I was persuaded to try and be a responsible adult and to think of my wife and children rather than my own pride of keeping myself out of jail.

They then accused me of being guilty of numerous terrorist activities. They read page after page from the file out to me and every page directly involved me in either a shooting or a bombing that took place in Enniskillen between the years 1971 and 1973. Although I knew that it was pointless telling them that I had never been involved in any such activity, I still continued to do so.

At no time did they refer to the terrible interview I had with them the previous Thursday night. Nor did I attempt to discuss it. I felt that I was getting an easy passage during this interview and I thought it would be better not to rock the boat.

At the conclusion of this interview, they both assured me that they would be remaining at Castlereagh for the rest of the day. If, during that time, I seriously considered my position as a responsible father and wished to make a statement, they would be only too willing to come to my assistance and help me to make it. They told me that I had only to ask any of the other detectives for them and they would be along immediately. I thanked them for their concern and they parted. I was really delighted to see them go, as I did not trust them. After this interview was over, I was brought back to the cell by the thinner of the two. He did not speak to me on the way back and just signed the book in the detention block. I was brought to my cell by the uniformed policemen on duty there.

During the short period back in my cell after this interview, I spent quite a while thinking over the sudden change of attitude towards me. I had again been interrogated by both pairs of detectives who had tortured me so severely during the interrogation sessions on Thursday night and Friday morning. Another factor which struck me as significant was that the dangers of getting out were being emphasised, particularly by the two who interviewed me on Monday morning. I tried not to get carried away with the idea that I might soon be released. I resorted back to my usual ritual of prayer and left my future in the hands of the Lord.

That afternoon I was again taken from my cell and brought back to interrogation room two. This time the two detectives who awaited me there were familiar to me, for they were both from Enniskillen. I knew one of them fairly well and it was he who began the interview. He began by telling me that he was very surprised to see me in Castlereagh and followed this with the comment that people were never brought to such a place for nothing. As he fingered through the file, which seemed to pass from one person to another with each fresh interview, he stared straight into my eyes and said, "Well, Bernie, you were either as white and innocent as that ceiling or as black in guilt as that floor, and you can take it from me that you're as black in guilt as that floor."

His elbows rested on the table. His chin was supported by the palm of his hands and he continued to stare straight at me. I did not reply. I was disgusted with his attitude. I had been glad to see that he was there to interview me for I felt that he was bound to know that I was not involved in any terrorist activities. I thought that he was going to tell me that I was going to be released. I just sat there and stared back at him. Our eyes were locked on each other. A long period of silence prevailed. His fellow interrogator, whom I remembered as a uniformed constable in Enniskillen about a year or two previously, sat to my right and looked at the both of us. No one moved and no one spoke. I stared on. Eventually, water began to appear in the eyes of my opponent. He was finding it difficult to maintain his stare. I was by this stage used to meeting the eyes of my interrogators, because some of them had told me that it was a sign of guilt if I was unable to look straight at them while I was being interviewed. In this instance, I proved their theory correct because my interviewer knew that he was wrong in accusing me of something that he knew to be untrue. He blinked and tears of embarrassment ran down his face.

His colleague, seeing the predicament he had landed himself in, changed the subject by asking me, "Mr O'Connor, what are your political beliefs?" I told him that I believed in a united Ireland. He continued to discuss politics for about an hour. We also chatted about the unions and the working of the Labour Party in England. By this time, the detective directly opposite me had got over his embarrassment and joined freely in the conversation. He was particularly talkative on the subject of education in the six counties. He talked of his son's progress at Portora Royal School, and compared it to other grammar schools in Enniskillen.

This interview lasted about two hours and, strangely enough, I was not accused of any terrorist involvement during the remainder of the interview. The initial outburst had been enough. I was told by my interrogators that they had been trained in their interview techniques in England. All interviewers had to do this course in order to be members of the Crime Squad team. One of the detectives who was conducting the interview told me that he was, in fact, just back from such a course.

At around half past five that Monday evening, I was returned to my cell for tea. By comparison to the other four days, Monday was passing along quite smoothly. No one was really putting pressure on me and the interviewers were all using the same advisory or fatherly role. I was finding it hard to understand because I had been expecting a rough passage sooner or later.

Tea arrived at around 6. It consisted of yet more beans, sausages, fried bread and chips. I had received this kind of meal so often now that the very sight of it turned me off. Even the policeman who served it to me noticed that I was not very keen. He told me that the police themselves had the same meal as the prisoners and that I would get used to them in time. I said that I did not like greasy food at the best of times, never mind when under the strain of being in such a place as this. He told me to eat as much as I could. I eventually managed most of the beans and a few chips but left the sausages. I was granted permission to get a beaker of water, which I used to get rid of the heavy taste of the fry from my mouth.

I spent the rest of the time in the cell praying very hard that I might be released. I kept counting the days that were left. I figured out that I would have to be released or charged on Wednesday, as my seven days would be up at 5 on Thursday morning. It would be most unlikely that I would be charged in the middle of the night, so therefore the court would be on Wednesday. I wondered what charge they would bring against me. I feared their use of unsigned statements which were written when they tried to involve me in the two murders. I reasoned with myself that they would not be so vicious as to concoct offences, but at other times I felt convinced of the opposite. One way or another, I felt that there would be only one more day's interrogation to come, leaving Wednesday for a court case.

22

INTERROGATION 20

After tea, I was again brought for interview. My interrogator for this session was a small, dark-haired, bearded detective who wore a blue suit. He was of course armed with my file. During the first few minutes of interview, he referred to a number of offences which according to the file I was alleged to have been involved in. I told him quite adamantly that I was innocent of any such involvement by thought, word, or deed. He was just as adamant that I had been involved. In fact, he became so annoyed that he glared at me angrily and shouted, "What do you mean, O'Connor? What you need is another bloody good hammering."

I didn't know if he was to be taken seriously or if he was just issuing an idle threat. I feared the former, owing to the malicious look on his face and the harshness of his voice. I tried to be as friendly and as pleasant to him as I could be. He continued to read to me from the file asking me to prove how it could be so wrong. Where I was alleged to have been involved in a certain explosion on a particular date and time, he demanded that I told him where exactly I had been at that point in time. This was practically impossible, as I was being asked to account for my movements at specific times four or five years ago. I tried to explain that I could not recall my movements a month back never mind five years. He refused to accept this argument and told me that all the PIRA members he had ever met gave him the same excuse.

As time went on, I became braver in my talk with him. I debated with him for about an hour on his ability to recognise when someone was telling the truth or not. He was very eager to prove himself in this respect. At the end of his rather weak theory on how he recognised the truth, I challenged him to come clean in relation to me. I suggested to him that if he was being really honest in what he claimed, he was bound to recognise that I was telling the truth. I asked him to read through all the notes which the previous interrogators had made concerning the interviews I had been through so far. I told him that he could see my consistency. I had been honest and truthful to everyone irrespective of the kind of treatment I had received.

His answer was short and to the point. He told me that intelligence briefs were drawn up by experts who acted on fact, and therefore I could not be telling the truth. At another stage of the interview, I asked him his name. He did not take too kindly to this request. He demanded in a loud, angry voice, "Do you think that I would give my name to a top Provo like you for you to have me done in?" I laughed. He said that it was no laughing matter. It was people like me who were pointing the finger at men like him so that they could be shot. From his attitude and his obvious emotional sincerity, I felt that he really believed what he was saying. I tried to convince him by being friendly and communicated that he was talking to an innocent man.

At around 8 p.m. that night, a familiar face appeared. It was that of the Enniskillen Chief Inspector. He was dressed in a tweed suit displaying his usual suave appearance. He dismissed the detective who was interviewing me in a breezy manner. Although I did not know what to expect from him, in a strange way, I was pleased to see him. Despite this, I was wary of expecting him as a friend after my experiences of the previous four days. He began by telling me that he was just another cog in the interrogation machine. He informed me that he could have arrested me years ago in Enniskillen for taking injured men across the border to hospital. But being a considerate and charitable man, he had hesitated. This was due, he claimed, to the fact that I was the father of seven children and also because of the active part I played in community work, especially with the youth in the area.

I was so disgusted with this kind of talk that I treated him with the contempt I felt that he deserved; I remained silent when he asked me to confess to his ridiculous accusations. When he realised that his 'know everything approach' was not working, he turned to being the friendly local inspector. He told me that my wife was most concerned about me and that he had done his best to console her. Eventually, after some time, he informed me that I was going to be released. I could scarcely believe my ears at this news. Early on he had given me the impression that I was going to be charged with some trumped up offence. I was very pleased that he was now giving me such good news.

A few minutes later, the Chief Superintendent came into the room. He was there in an official capacity to inform me that I was due for release and that a doctor was going to examine me. I suggested that this was unnecessary but was told that it was part of the procedure of release to have a medical examination.

I spent a while waiting for the medical examination. I discussed with the two high ranking officers the different series of interrogations I had come through. I made sure I referred to the detectives that had physically abused me and told them that they should be removed. The Superintendent asked me if I had anything good to say about some of the interrogators. I told them that I understood that detectives have a job to do and some of them did that in a professional manner but some of them were unfit for purpose. The conversation came around to the visit of my doctor on Saturday afternoon. The Chief Superintendent referred to him as a "country quack who would not know what a bruise was." I refused to comment.

He went on to say that it was unlikely that suspected terrorists could begin to make confessions in Castlereagh without being "first shook up a little." He described the treatment which I had received as being a little "roughed up." He referred to the bruises on my face and chest, which my doctor had made a report on, as being "trivial and insignificant."

Eventually, a uniformed policeman came into the room and announced that a doctor had arrived to examine me. On leaving the Superintendent, I offered to shake his hand, but he refused. I was taken to the medical room and there I met a young fair-haired doctor. He referred to the fact that I had already had a medical examination a few days previously and asked, "Have you anything further to say about being in Castlereagh since you were last medically examined?"

"No," I replied.

"Do you want a full examination now?" he continued. As nothing further had happened to me since my examination on the previous Saturday, I said no. I then signed the relevant form for him, and I was brought to the office where I had my possessions taken from me on my arrival that first Thursday morning. I was given back my watch and laces, medal and chain, a £1 note and a number of items which had not been brought to me in the interrogation centre. The uniformed sergeant at the desk informed me that these extra items had been sent to the detention centre by my wife. I signed for the items and was brought back to the interrogation room.

I met the Enniskillen CI there and he offered to drive me to my home in Enniskillen. I accepted the lift home. The conversation going home was very much about cars, school, community work in Enniskillen and nothing was mentioned about Castlereagh, acts of terrorism or politics. I even slept for a while with the heat on in his car.

Statement of Dr George Dennis Johnston, Medical Practitioner, City Hospital,
Taken by Chief Inspector Brown at his home on 23 February 1977

On the 24 January 1977 I was called to the Police Office at Castlereagh to

examine Bernard O'Connor who was being released from detention.

At 9pm O'Connor was brought into the Medical Room where I saw him alone. I

asked him to be seated. The door was closed and the Police Officer who had

brought him to me was in the other room. I commenced to fill out the Police

Medical Form 38/17(b) by deleting the words Initial and Intermediate at the

top, indicating that this was now the final examination. I then asked Mr

O'Connor for his name and address and his date of birth, all of which I

recorded on the top of the Form. I then asked Mr O'Connor was he alleging

assault or ill treatment while in the Holding Centre. He replied "No".

I then deleted the appropriate words on the form to correspond with his

answer. I asked him then did he wish to be medically examined to which he

also replied, "No". I then asked Mr O'Connor to sign the form under the

answers he had just given. I then asked the Constable from the next room to

come in and he also signed the form witnessing Mr O'Connor's signature in

Mr O'Connor's presence. I then completed the form at the bottom giving the

time of finish of examination as 9.10pm and signed the form there.

During my interview with Mr O'Connor I was not aware of any bruising on the parts

of him that I could see. My impression was that he was relaxed and showed no

sign of mental stress. My recollection of his movement while walking into and

from the medical room was that it was a normal gait and if it had been otherwise

I would have made reference to it.

I did not use the word "full" when asking Mr O'Connor if he wished to be

medically examined. I gave Mr O'Connor no reason to believe that my questions

regarding allegations of assault or ill treatment only referred to a time since

his examination by his own doctor. I did not know in fact that he had received such

an examination. My question referred specifically to the time he had been

detained at the Holding Centre and not for a part of that period only.

(Signed) Dennis Johnston MB D.CH. MRCP

Compared with original statement and certified to be a true copy thereof

100 _____ Inspector

FORM 38/17(b)

Medical Examination (Initial/Intermediate/Final) at .... Castlereagh Holding Cutre ....

Police Station on (date) ...... 25th .... (time) .... 9.00 pm ....

Name ...... O'Connor Bernard ...... Address ...... 38 Willoughby Place Enniskillin

Date of Birth ...... 21 · 6 · 42 ·

I, ... Bernard O'Connor ...... wish/do not wish to be medically examined.

I am/am not alleging assault or ill-treatment.

Signed ...... B O'Connor .... Witness .... T. Harvey ....

I agree/ do not agree to whatever medical treatment may be thought desirable.

Signed .... Signature of Examining MO ...... Ennis Johnston ......

Witness .... Date ...... 24 · 1 · 77 ...... Time ...... 9·10 pm ......

COMPLAINT CERTIFICATE

TO BE COMPLETED PRIOR TO PRISONER/SUSPECT LEAVING STATION/P.O.

Have you any complaints to make against any Police Officer while you were detained in Police custody?

I have been asked by Sergt/~~Const~~ _T. Armstrong_ If I have any complaints to make against any Police Officer while

detained in police custody from _9.05_ am/~~pm~~ on

the _20/1/77_ to _9.15_ ~~am~~/pm on the

_24/1/77_

* My reply is _Complaint made to Doctor_

SIGNED _B. O'Connor_
(Prisoner)

SIGNED _____
(A.S.D.O./Gaoler)

SIGNED _____
(Witness)

*This portion should be completed by Prisoner/Suspect

Bernard O'Connor   D.O.B. 21/6/42

es 38 Willoughby Plan, Enniskillen   OCCUPATION:: Electrician

informed on being taken into police custody at 9.05 a.m./p.m. on

/77 at Castlereagh Police Office that I had been arrested by a constable

Section 12 of the Prevention of Terrorism (Temporary Provisions) Act 1976 on

mable suspicion of being concerned/having been concerned/in the commission,

ration or instigation of acts of terrorism.

informed that any request or complaint about my treatment when in custody should
de to an Inspector of the R.U.C. or to any other policemen as soon as possible.

TS (if any) _____ Yes _____

ollowing is a complete list of my property which was taken from me by the
e.

| added 3.45Pm 22/1/77 |
| Newspaper (Fermanagh News) |
| 2 Novels (Saint in August, SEAN) |
| Glasses in Scalbbed |
| 4 Bars bloc |
| 1 Shirt Victory V Bazagin |
| 20 buigs |

ture X B O'Connor   Date 20/1/77   Time 9.05 am

Bernard O'Connor   ADDRESS 38 WILLOUGHBY PLACE
                            ENNISKILLEN

fy that during the time I was held "in arrest" at Castlereagh Police Office, I
properly treated and had no injuries inflicted on me by anyone.

have no complaints to make

wish to make the following complaint Complaint made to Dctiv.

so certify that all the property listed above was returned to me (with the
tion of)*

ture B O'Connor.   Date 24/1/77   Time 9.15P.17

lete as appropriate.

23

BACK IN ENNISKILLEN
24TH JANUARY

Meanwhile in Enniskillen, my wife was having a tough time. Here is her account for Monday 24th. On Monday morning I phoned Castlereagh and was told that there was still no change. Father Mullan arrived and told me that he had been trying to get in touch with the Chief Inspector at Enniskillen, but had been told that he had gone to Belfast. I said that the Chief Inspector had gone to Belfast to bring him home.

Doctor Brennan arrived to examine Phillip and told me that if he hadn't improved by three o'clock, he would put him into hospital. I felt completely shattered and helpless and wondered what I could do. I felt that my son's condition was due to his daddy's arrest. After two I went up the town to see our solicitor. As soon as I sat down, I started to cry and implored him to do something. I told him that Dr Mulhern had told me about the abuse and I told him that I hadn't told anyone except Eamonn and Father Mullen. I felt I was going mental with worrying. He phoned Castlereagh while I was there and requested to see his client. On being refused, he asked that they record the time of his request. He then phoned Dr Mulhern and had a conversation with him. He then phoned a colleague in Belfast. He told me that he would start work right away on two possibilities: one, what he would do if Barney was charged; two, what he would do if Barney was released. I can't remember how long I spent there, but when I got home Phil had stopped vomiting and was able to keep down a little water. I continued to phone Castlereagh about every hour. Still no change. At about half past seven, Brother Peter, Bernard's headmaster, phoned to tell me that when he had phoned Castlereagh a few minutes earlier, he was told that there was a possibility that Barney was being released. I phoned immediately but could not get any confirmation of this. Mrs Maguire phoned and told me that she had been told of the same possibility. I again phoned Castlereagh and said that if Bernie was being released that he would not require police transport home. I asked that I be informed if he was being released and that our own car would go for him. At nine o'clock, Fr Mullen phoned. He told me that he had received a call from Castlereagh to say that Bernie was on his way home with the Chief Inspector. I replaced the phone and cried my eyes out. When I had calmed down, I spent the next hour phoning friends to pass on the good news. I went upstairs to talk to Phillip, who had not slept all day, and told him that his daddy would soon be home. Before I got to the door, Phil was fast asleep. About half past 10, there were about 12 people in the house with me. A neighbour had called at the door to inquire about Barney. As I was talking to him, two cars came up the street and turned. The first stopped on the far side just passed our house and the second stopped almost facing the house. The first car then drove on and out of the second stepped Barney and Chief Inspector Curry. They both came across the road and I met them on the footpath. I remember saying to Chief Inspector Curry that I knew "Santa" would bring him home. CI Curry came into the home and joined the crowd in the sitting room and had some supper. The phone rang constantly. Dr Mulhern phoned and arranged that he would call. Barney was laughing and chatting nonstop. He appeared to have lost about a stone in weight, and his eyes were very glassy and protruding. When he walked, his legs were very badly bent. After CI Curry left, he started to tell us what had happened to him since he had left home on the Thursday morning. His language, when he was telling it, was foul and every so often, he would say to Fr Mullen, "Sorry father. But that's the way they spoke to me in Castlereagh." As I listened, I was stunned. This wasn't abuse: this was torture. The record that the RUC had taken from my home on that dreaded morning was called 'The Price of Justice', and as I looked at my husband I knew that he had paid just that, the price of justice.

After everyone had gone, except Gerry and Agnes, we made more tea and I can remember as Barney tried to hold the cup and saucer, it rattled so much that I took the saucer from him as I was afraid that the cup was going to fall over. He then had a bath. He was talking nonstop to me. We eventually went up to the bedroom. We got into bed, but after a few minutes he got up and went to look at the two boys and little Aine. He cried as he went around them. He spent the whole night walking about.

On Thursday I insisted he stayed in bed. The doctor came and examined him. The solicitor called as did some friends. He ate a little lunch but still could not sleep. After teatime, he got up for a while. I had noticed during the doctor's examination that his chest had bruise marks and he had the remains of a black eye. The inside of both ears were jet black. They looked as if someone had put soot in them. He still had that very lazy stare and his eyes were protruding; as he talked, when looking at whoever he was talking to, he was unsteady all the time. That night he slept for a short time. This was the first time since the terrible banging of the front door on that terrible Thursday morning that he slept. After a few days, he started to unwind. He seemed to shake. Sometimes, he got very stroppy. He had difficulty getting in and out of bed or even the armchair. He had difficulty walking. He was very quiet at times over the following days. Then, suddenly, he was very edgy, and sometimes, very vicious. I had to keep the children out of his way on those occasions. This man was not the same person.

appears we can take him at his word".

Apart from the human rights issue, one of the matters the caucus leaders raised with the

the United Nations Committee on Human Rights at Geneva, after he had been nominated by the Irish National Caucus in the U.S.

stein mentioned Ireland in particular.

"This is seen as a marked departure from previous American policy" said Mr. McManus.

Police centre probe urged by Dr. Daly

THE Bishop of Derry, Most Rev. Edward Daly yesterday called for a total review of all statements taken over the past six months at the RUC Castlereagh holding centre in Belfast, because of allegations of torture there. But the Police Federation of Northern Ireland yesterday criticised last week's BBC TV programme Tonight, in which torture allegations were made, as trial by TV, and " a biased trial at that".

Dr. Daly called for the review because of the "grave concern" of many people following the allegations of torture at the centre by two men made during the Tonight programme last Wednesday.

He said that the allegations Mr. Bernard O'Connor (34), Fermanagh schoolteacher and Michael Lavelle, a factory worker, substantiated quite a number of allegations which had been brought to his attention recently.

He added that in a situation described by the two men, many people would "cave-in" and sign statements admitting something which they may not be guilty of.

It raises the spectre of Palace Barracks, Strasbourg and Compton, all over again" said Dr. Daly on the RTE programme This Week.

He added that he did not believe the incidents described by the two men were isolated, and from evidence he had relied, he had been concerned for some time.

Dr. Daly said that he did not know if such torture methods were used with the knowledge of the authorities, to my mind, it is the mark of a civilised people that methods of governments are civilised, even under provocation."

Complaining that safeguards built into the "seven days process, which would be visits by doctors and solicitors each day, if any, meant that this would stop officers from using

BBC will meet union on 'blacking'

THE BBC will meet officers of the technicians' union, the Association of Broadcasting Staffs, in London today to discuss their blacking of the Northern Ireland programme Spotlight on Friday night.

The ABS blacked the programme because, they said, an interview with a member of a body calling itself the Irish National Liberation Army screened last week put at risk the lives of its members.

A statement from the BBC said that its paramount concern was for the safety of its staff, consistent with its obligations under the law.

said they were trying to prevent the establishment of new industries in the North.

" I cannot set what they want to achieve by it. Whatever situation emerges in the North we are going to need industry and jobs."

Dr. Daly added that there were signs that the IRA was beginning to realise the futility of its campaign, but he agreed with the opinion of Dr. Cathal Daly that while the IRA could not win, it could not be completely defeated either.

allegations until their investigations have been completed.

The chairman of the Police Federation of Northern Ireland, Mr. Alan Wright, said that in view of the official investigation they could not at this stage comment on specific allegations contained in the programme.

But the federation nevertheless "deplored the grossly unfair nature of the programme, which was broadcast with full prior knowledge by the BBC that the police could not participate for very proper reasons," he said.

The programme bore all the hallmarks of trial by television, the statement said, adding "and a biased trial at that".

People would wonder and rightly so, the statement went on, at the difference in treatment accorded to the two men interviewed in the programme and the treatment "to which police officers feel themselves subjected when they are interviewed on television.

" Programmes of this nature, at this time, are very likely to encourage further assaults and atrocities against the police who are endeavouring to serve the community," said the statement.

It then posed this question: "When the next police officer suffers the ultimate brutality of being murdered, will the BBC show a thirty second clip of film in passing, or will they mount an extended national programme showing the suffering and grief of 99 police families and widows'?

"Secondly, in view

Fermanagh Men's Police Torture Claims

"Malicious Propaganda"
West Protests to BBC

The War In Ulst

"War Plan" To Beat Assassins

"Resign," Maguire MP Tells Chief Constable

10 March 1977

25p

The Listener

USA AND CANADA 75c

Interrogation: what Bernard O'Connor claimed on 'Tonight'

VOL 97 NO 2499

Eugene Marais: page 298

Contents

Keith Kyle

Bernard O'Connor's story

'The authorities are now placing first priority on picking up the organisers of IRA violence. This is an altogether admirable policy, but Bernard O'Connor's account of his interrogation raises the question of whether or not it has sometimes involved inadmissible means'

For some 40 minutes on Wednesday of last week, a 34-year-old Enniskillen schoolmaster, called Bernard O'Connor, spoke on the *Tonight* programme (BBC1) of his experiences when being questioned by the police at Castlereagh Holding Centre in Belfast. What he described was not quite the same as the sensory deprivation techniques which had just been the subject of a solemn pledge by the attorney-general, Mr Sam Silkin, at Strasbourg. They had been used in 1971 and before, but Mr Silkin told the European Court of Human Rights that they had never been used since and that they would never be used in the future.

There was no mention by Mr O'Connor of 'white' noise, for example, and although he alleges both hooding and being forced to stand in awkward positions, which resemble the methods repudiated in the Silkin pledge, these were not sustained. It would appear, for anything like the extraordinary lengths of time that occurred in 1971. Nor, though, some of his interrogations went on most of the night, and one he estimates, lasted for 12 hours, would it be true to say that he was deliberately deprived of all food and sleep.

Nevertheless, the findings against Britain of 'cruel and inhuman treatment' by the Human Rights Commission, whose report

precedes the opening of a case in the Court, related to a wider range of practices than those covered by the pledge. Within this range, Bernard O'Connor's allegations seem to fit, so that the programme that we have put out does raise, quite squarely, the question of whether inadmissible practices are being currently used in Northern Ireland. It relates also to the question of whether, as the British lawyers allege, the Irish government ought to have been satisfied by the pledges made to it and is being merely obtuse in continuing with the case.

BBC producer James Thomason and I came across this story by chance. We were in Enniskillen filming the Fermanagh district council in session, as part of a report discussing the Macrory plan for reducing the missing upper tier of local government. A local councillor asked me for a private interview, and brought Bernard O'Connor to see me. He told me of his experiences, but no mention was made of television. It was a week later that we put that idea to him and it was only after prolonged discussion, involving his solicitor, that he agreed to appear on the screen.

He had already put the Saturday following the Monday of his release dictated a full account into his solicitor's dictaphone which formed the basis of the 21-page brief

which accompanied his formal complaint to the RUC of abusive treatment. A week later, two representatives of the RUC's complaints branch interviewed him at his solicitor's office. According to the solicitor, the two officers went through the 21-page brief line by line, asking O'Connor to expand on one point after another. On all points he was able to do so.

Bernard O'Connor is a slight (5ft 6in and nine stone), energetic man going prematurely bald, with a wife and seven children, ranging in age from ten years to two months. They live in a roomy, elegant house near the centre of Enniskillen. Besides being a teacher in the Catholic primary school, he runs with a partner, the only driving school in the town. He was once a salaried youth officer of the community centre, but has given that up for voluntary youth work, which he does on quite a considerable scale. He is in the choral society and is known in the Roman Catholic community of Enniskillen as a man generous with his time and talent, a good citizen. He also possesses, as viewers last week might have concluded, a remarkable memory and an ordinary power of self-expression. We filmed altogether about two hours of his account. It had, of course, to be heavily edited in the power of shortened before transmission, but it conveyed, I think, the spirit of the original.

It started at 5.30am of Thursday 20 January this year, with a very loud banging on his front door. Outside were a large number of army men who had come to search his house, and police who had come to arrest him under Section 12 of the Prevention of Terrorism Act. That section enables a person to be held without charge

18 March 1977 25p USA & Canada $1.00 Air

NEW STATESMAN

SPRING BOOKS

Wilfred Beckerman
What No-Growth Society?

Reports from India, Pakistan, Bangladesh
University Forum: York Under Siege
John Carey: What Exactly Do You Mean?
V. S. Pritchett: Shakespeare the Opportunist
Clive James   Jeremy Isaacs   Martin Amis

Nws 4
N112
LGS

Mr Mason and Mr O'Connor

'I was made to stand on my toes with my knees in a bent position and my hands out in front of me for three or four hours.' It is necessary to quote the words in which Mr Bernard O'Connor, an Enniskillen teacher, described his experiences while in the custody of the Royal Ulster Constabulary because the truth or otherwise of his account does not appear to be a central issue in the eyes of Mr Roy Mason, Secretary of State for Northern Ireland. 'A tracksuit was taken by one of the interviewers and put down over my head and tied around my neck in hood style, and then my nose was blocked off and my mouth was blocked off by their hands through the tracksuit. I fainted, maybe for half a minute, maybe for five minutes.' One policeman, says Mr O'Connor, 'insisted on punching me to the back of the head while he held the front of my forehead. He would punch me until I felt his knuckles were getting too sore.' Another policeman 'insisted on punching me to the stomach at regular intervals.' After 17 hours of continuous interrogation, Mr O'Connor was seen by a doctor, who states that his examination leads to the conclusion that the man 'had been assaulted while in police custody'. Mr O'Connor went on to assert that he was ordered by RUC men to confess to terrorist activities – in legal terms to conspiracy to murder – and told that he or members of his family would be killed if he refused to do so. In fact, he has not been charged with any such offences.

This was the story told by Mr O'Connor to a BBC interviewer, and brought to the television screen in a now famous *Tonight* programme. Mr Mason has strongly criticised the BBC for transmitting the interview, and his attack has been reinforced by senior officers of the constabulary. Their attitude is understandable; they are combatants in a bitter and often disheartening contest against the IRA, and they react angrily against anything that adds to their difficulties. The Secretary of State's position is different. In conditions of direct rule, he is in effect the Governor of the Province. He has to earn confidence in his integrity from the people, Catholic as well as Protestant.

Basically, he has no relation to the political appeal in Northern Ireland. It is for the great majority of the Province that this is not merely for him, but also for things of an indefinite duration to really worry about of issues that are more or less.

Mr Mason has chosen, of his own volition and indeed gratuitously, to launch a vendetta against the British media of information and the BBC in particular. He has therefore lost trust and respect both in Britain and abroad and gained only minded people in Britain. Although he denies that he seeks to institute a censorship, he clearly wishes to keep silent about a situation in which his treatment of the press are not publicised. The important issue is his attitude and his freedom in the journalistic sphere. He has had a disgraceful reputation ever in France and indeed in the world. For independence from government authority. At this time of Suez, for instance, it stood firm against strong pressure to suppress awkward facts and unwelcome comment. This is a question immensely valuable, but only in France, Britain or South Africa believe that the BBC was too weak and they believe it because they have some influence. It is away only at great risk. For standing up to Mr Mason the Director-General deserves nothing but applause.

The other issue is the less critical. Certain practices are outlawed by the conventions of civilised mankind, and admit of no excuse. Torture may vary, but the practices already meted out to Mr O'Connor is certainly of a kind with that which has earned Britain the condemnation of the European Commission on Human Rights, and which is repeated. Informed opinion in Europe and America has ceased to see the IRA as a liberation movement or to imagine that the Ulster problem can be simply resolved, but is very far from imagining Britain's hands to be entirely clean. What was wrong in Algeria and Vietnam is wrong in Ulster. That includes the torture.

Bernard O'Connor making his torture claims in B.B.C.'s 'Tonight' programme

Torture Claims The Media Have Ignored

By Eamonn McCann

THE CLASH between the B.B.C. on the one hand and Roy Mason, Airey Neave and the R.U.C. on the other, over the broadcasting of allegations by two men that they had been tortured in Castlereagh R.U.C. station, has obscured the real issue. The case vigorously advanced against the B.B.C. is that, by publicising an isolated case which is still under investigation the programme unfairly besmirched the reputation and damaged the morale of the R.U.C. as a whole. There has followed a heady debate about the responsibilities of the media in a "war situation." But the allegations only appeared isolated because the media has long been in dereliction of duty by failing to look into similar stories told by dozens of men, and some women, after interrogation by R.U.C. detectives.

At 7 a.m. on October 27th, 1976, Irwin O'Neill (21), Martin Cassidy (25) and Joseph Hunter (23), all of Kireen, Co. Derry, were questioned about recent assassinations in the area. O'Neill says that over a period of six hours he was held against a wall and punched in the stomach, then put in a chair with his head pulled back by the hair while being punched around the body. Cassidy says he was slapped, punched, kicked, made to stand spread-eagled against a wall while detectives kicked at him from behind and "pushed (his) face into the wall." Hunter says he was made to stand with arms outstretched and knees bent for a long period, then to hold his hands high in the air while spun around by a number of detectives until he was dizzy; that he was then thrown from one detective to another, then "bounced off the wall," held by his knees by one detective while another punched and slapped him around the ears, and told it would not be difficult to have him assassinated in Coleraine or Upper [...]

Seamus Doherty (31), Peter Doherty and Brian Grugan (26), from the Coalisland area, were arrested around [...] on November 22nd, brought to [...] Road barracks in Derry, and questioned about I.R.A. activity in south [...] Seamus Doherty says he was hit around the ears and punched in the kidneys; that one detective held him by the throat while another punched in the stomach; that a detective [...] him by the hair and swung him [...] the room while another stood [...] at him; that he was spread [...] against a wall while detectives [...] him between the legs from behind; [...] told: "There's only one thing for boys—the bullet in the head."

Peter Doherty says he was punched in the face and stomach, knocked to the ground and pulled up again by the hair, put in a "sitting position" and punched and kicked, made to do press-ups and by the hair while pulled by the hair while his face, head banged against the wall, told: "You work no cycle in Coleraine. It would not be hard to touch you sit down there, it's the right company for it." Grugan says he was made to do press-ups held by the hair and his head banged against the wall many times, punched in the stomach, kicked in the testicles; that he was stripped naked and that detectives then "laughed and joked about my body", that water was poured over his head and into his ears.

Fintan Mullin (20), Kevin Mallon (33), Gerard Farren (24) and Kieran Farren (21), all of Dungiven, were arrested between 6 a.m. and 7 a.m. on December 1st and taken to Castlereagh. All say they were denied to indulge in any one of a selection of crimes recently committed around Dungiven. Fintan Mullin says he was punched, kneed in the testicles and pulled around a room by the hair for up to two hours. Kevin Mallon says he was threatened, thrown around a room, that one detective held him by the throat, applying pressure, while another punched him around the body. Gerard Farren says he was knocked to the ground, kicked in the stomach, dragged around a room by the hair, made to stand for a long period with arms outstretched and knees buckled, threatened that a live wire would be stuck on his anus. Kieran Farren says he was knocked to the ground, pulled by the hair, punched, kicked, made to stand with arms outstretched, legs apart and knees bent. Every time one man fell I was punched in the groin and stomach. If I straightened up I was then kicked down at the knees until they bent again."

Noel McCloskey, Thomas Donaghey and David Ward, of Dungiven, were [...]

O'Connor to sue RUC chief for 'torture'

THE Director of Public Prosecutions in Belfast is taking no action against policemen at Castlereagh interrogation centre in the case of Mr. Bernard O'Connor, who said he was tortured.

The Fermanagh teacher alleged torture by R.U.C. men, and caused a sensation when an interview with him was broadcast by the BBC earlier this year.

The file on the case has been with the DPP's office for some months and was returned within the last few days to the R.U.C. without any recommendation of action against the police officers alleged to be involved in treating Mr. O'Connor brutally.

The decision, which became known yesterday, is certain to cause a political storm in the North, where allegations are being made weekly that the police in Castlereagh are using brutal measures to get statements and confessions from suspects stealing from Mount Mellenay, Co. Waterford, where

he is attending the Jamborara International Scout Camp, Mr. O'Connor said last that he had already instructed his solicitor to issue proceedings against the Chief Constable of the RUC.

Mr. O'Connor's initial reaction to the news of the decision was a shake of the head and the comment: " It's exactly what was to be expected ".

He revealed, however, that only last weekend, before he left for the Camp, he had instructed his solicitor in Enniskillen, Mr. Tony McGettigan, to prosecute the Chief Constable for illegal arrest, torture and malicious injury. " I had set a deadline for a response to my complaint," he said, " and when that passed, I told my solicitor to go ahead.

In the television interview, with BBC reporter Keith Kyle, Mr. O'Connor claimed that

amnesty international

International Secretariat, 10 Southampton Street, London WC2E 7HF, England
Telephone: 01-836 7788 Telegrams: Amnesty London Telex: 28502

dk/vn   12 March 1979

trobsni

EXPRESS
P.J. Flanagan & Co.
Solicitors
11 Town Hall Street
Enniskillen, Co. Fermanagh
BT74 7BD
Northern Ireland

Dear Mr. Flanagan,

Re.: Bernard O'Connor -v- Chief Constable R.U.C.

Thank you for your letter of 22 January 1979. Enclosed please
find the medical report on Mr. O'Connor, drawn up by Amnesty International's
medical doctors. I must draw your attention to their covering letter and
would like to stress again that the first part of the report contains
allegations which can be corroborated only to the extent that they are
consistent generally with the pattern of maltreatment as established by
our 1978 Report, and specifically with our medical findings. Amnesty
International's medical doctors have direct knowledge only of their own
detailed examination described in the second part of the report (from
page 7, 'Physical examination done on Dec. 5, 1977').

Please keep us informed of developments.

                                   Yours sincerely,

                                   Dick Oosting
                                   Deputy Secretary General

24

POLICE COMPLAINTS COMMISSION

While under arrest in Castlereagh, I had been afraid to make any complaints of ill treatment for fear it could harm my prospects of release or even my life – a concern given weight by a remark I later heard reported from a senior police officer who commented, in an unguarded moment, "It's not that it really happened. He [Bernard] should not have had the chance to tell it." But the day after my release I began the procedure of making a formal complaint through the Police Complaints Commission. My solicitor, Tony McGettingan of the Enniskillen firm Flanagan and Company, came to my house on 28th January and I made detailed statements describing every stage of my interrogation, in the terms detailed in the previous chapters. It amounted to some 30 pages. I read through and signed it five days later. Two members of the RUC's Complaints and Disciplines Branch, officers Hood and Brown, then came to his office to interview me and went through my accounts, line by line. These men would later appear in court on a daily basis during my civil case against the force.

I received communications telling me my complaint was being investigated; then, on 28th July, some six months later, I had a very brief letter telling me my case had been rejected due to "insufficient evidence to prosecute." I was not surprised – my solicitor had forewarned me of the inevitable outcome but vowed there and then to take legal action against the police. A civil case was the only option left to me.

When I first met my senior QC, Charles Hill, at the Chichester Street courts in Belfast, I was entering the unknown. He questioned whether "an insignificant little bastard" like myself could hope to take on the might of the establishment and win, when no one else had succeeded. Provocative words, but indicative that he had done his homework. This was the exact same derogatory phrase used by one of my most vicious interrogators in Castlereagh. It was this meticulous research and attention to minutiae of detail that was to characterise the success of his representation and cross-examination. Tony McGettigan had secured the services of the right man.

Meanwhile, my case had attracted unexpected international attention due to the intervention of an investigative journalist, Keith Kyle. He and his producer Janine Thomason were working for the BBC on a series of reports on the vastly reduced powers of local councils – the much vaunted "bogs, bins and burials" – and had decided to concentrate on two council areas where gerrymandering was rife, Derry and Fermanagh. My local SDLP councillor Jim Donnelly, the same man who would later try to persuade me to stand for the party, had mentioned to them the case of a local schoolteacher who had suffered very serious abuse under interrogation in Castlereagh, and they asked to meet me. I discussed this with my solicitor; I was in two minds. Might the BBC take a very British stance on the matter? Might it turn out to be to my detriment? I was fearful it could endanger me or my family. I agreed to meet them at the Killyhevlin Hotel, where we talked for four hours. They were clearly very keen. I later found out they had had briefings from influential figures including the Bishop of Derry and Dr Edward Daly, himself a native of Belleek. They had also used their sources to speak to senior Republican figures in the south, and to the Republic's Minister for Foreign Affairs, Dr Garrett Fitzgerald.

I agreed to a second meeting at my home, in the presence of my solicitor Tony McGettigan. An agreement was drawn up whereby I would have the right to see the finished documentary before it was broadcast, and to have it withdrawn if I was unhappy with it. On this basis, I agreed to proceed. We then spent a full day filming, on 25th February. Both sides were very, very cautious in their approach to such potentially explosive material. Keith and Janine had been liaising with their controller, Dick Francis, who, despite not inconsiderable opposition from more conservative and Unionist influences, stood fast to his decision to broadcast across the UK. I had been heartened throughout the process by Keith Kyle's stated position: "This is not British justice and it shouldn't be allowed to happen."

The film was broadcast on 2nd March 1977, and caused havoc among the British establishment. I was headline news. The film was optioned for educational purposes for French law students and featured in Open University courses for years to come.

The programme had its own international legacy. Lord Bennett began his investigation of the north's interrogation centres, including Castlereagh, and later published his damning findings in the Bennett Report. In 1998, Keith sent me the following letter and extract from a lecture he delivered at the University of Ulster.

25 Oppidans Road,
London NW3 3AG
0171-586-1903

6 August 1998

Bernard O'Connor,Esq.,
38 Willoughby Place,
Enniskillen,
Co.Fermanagh,
Northern Ireland.

Dear Bernie,

It was a great pleasure to see you again after all
these years and Suzy, who heard so much about you at the time,
was delighted to have the chance of meeting you.

I was, of course, interested to hear all your news,
especially about your professional advancement and about your
transatlantic achievements with the scout band. The sample we
saw of your family gave us an idea of just how charming and well-
brought up they are. It was depressing though to hear that you
still have trouble with some of the local police and the one
incident that you described was deeply disturbing. Your morale,
however, seems to be high and, in the circumstances, your good
spirits are an example to us all.

When reminiscing with you about the events of 1977 I
mentioned that they had featured in a lecture I gave at the
University of Ulster about my experiences as a television
journalist during the first decade of the Troubles. The lecture
was included in a book called <u>Broadcasting in a Divided Community</u>
which was published by the Institute of Irish Studies at The
Queen's University Belfast. I thought you might be interested to
see it, so I am enclosing a photocopy.

I wish you and your entire family every success in all
your endeavours.

Yours

Keith Kyle

The most controversial programme with which I was associated in Ireland was the Bernard O'Connor interview. Bernard O'Connor was a school teacher and driving instructor in Enniskillen. He is an outspoken Republican and in 1969 at the time of the early civil rights agitation when he was an active member of the People's Democracy, he ran a small, rather cheeky magazine which had offended members of the local power elite in Fermanagh, Catholic as well as Protestant. He also – which is of crucial importance to this story – has remarkable powers of total recall. I had not gone to Enniskillen in 1977 with the purpose of meeting him. On the contrary I was going on a rather low-key story about the new local councils. In intervals of filming the Fermanagh Council in action, I was persistently lobbied by one of its SDLP members to talk to a man who had been discharged by the police after undergoing interrogation at the Castlereagh barracks. I was in a hurry, I was not investigating the RUC, and was very leery of allegations which, up to then, seemed to come exclusively from Sinn Féin. The councillor was importunate, and I agreed to see his man for a few minutes.

My initial impression of O'Connor was favourable and I immediately realised that he would make a natural for television: precise, coherent, fluent, intelligible. That meant that if the BBC put him on the screen, he would probably carry conviction; to me that made the responsibility involved in putting him on at all that much greater. Moreover, I had a great deal of sympathy for the predicament of the RUC. I had not had a long enough conversation with O'Connor to reach any conclusion and, in any case, the final decision would not be mine. When we returned to London, my producer, Janine Thomason, recommended to the editor of Tonight that we take up the story and after some initial hesitation this was tentatively agreed. I was sent back without a crew to make further enquiries. Janine and I spent altogether seven hours with O'Connor and a great deal more with people who could throw light on his personality, background, and activities. It seemed established that he was not connected with Sinn Féin or any other political party since his days with the PDs. He had been detained on suspicion of being a 'godfather' of the IRA but after a week's interrogation at Castlereagh they had had to release him (and, I may say, nothing has been found against him since). He insisted that he enjoyed good relations with members of the uniformed police and that he had nothing against them, though he did admit that in the early, hectic days of peaceful demonstration, when the only violence came from the other side, he had once said, 'The only good policeman is a dead policeman.'

Bernard O'Connor's interrogation, by his own account, was in every respect abusive – immensely long overnight sessions without a break, interrogation while obliged to undress and to be subjected to various forms of acute physical stress, punching in the ribs, demeaning physical acts, endless insults relating to his religion and his family and threats, such as that if he were released it would be onto the Shankill Road with the UVF alerted as to when he would be there. It immediately struck me that the acts described appeared to coincide with the lesser of the two categories of 'inhuman and degrading treatment' in respect of which the British Government had been found guilty by the European Human Rights Commission at Strasbourg. As it happened, when driving to Enniskillen, before we had spoken to O'Connor, Janine and I had heard on the car radio that the Attorney-General, Sam Silkin, had given Britain's word that all acts complained of by the Irish Government (which has brought the Strasbourg case) had been completely ended, that there was no question of recurrence, and that, therefore, Britain should be let off the final stage of a Strasbourg case, prosecution before the Human Rights Court.

Informally I laid the details of O'Connor's allegations before the late Sir James Fawcett, then the chairman of the European Human Rights Commission, and he confirmed to me that he would consider the case, if shown to be genuine, as falling directly under the rubric of cruel, inhuman and degrading treatment. It was this, really, that made me feel that it was right to proceed with a television film.

I decided that the really remarkable thing about O'Connor's testimony was its meticulous completeness; he had the gift of total recall; he had his interrogations precisely timed (he said he was able to read a wristwatch upside down); the appearance, dress and mood of each interrogator were exactly detailed; the sequence of exchanges between him and each interrogator was vividly laid out. It was apparent that if an accurate impression were to be given of his story that he should have much more time than a usual *Tonight* item and that his presence and manner were sufficient to hold the attention of an audience for a longer period. The Editor of *Tonight* sent Janine Thomason and me with a crew to interview O'Connor, without any guarantee of subsequent transmission and we came back with over an hour of material.

I recommended that the Director-General's permission be sought – this was not technically essential because no one had suggested that O'Connor was literally a member of the IRA (and he expressed disapproval of its violent methods) but I was pretty certain that we should run into some political trouble and I thought that if the D-G was going to be in at the crash landing it was only fair to him that he should be there at the takeoff. He appointed two very senior figures, both now dead, one of them the late Sir Richard Francis, who was by now the Belfast Region Controller, to see the film and advise him. When they had seen it, they told me that they believed that Bernard O'Connor was telling the truth. They said, however, that transmission should be postponed a fortnight to give the Chief Constable of the RUC more notice and to give me a chance to go back to Enniskillen and to put on film some of the surrounding research I had got in my notebook, including an interview with O'Connor's doctor who had examined him while in detention and had found worrying traces of ill-treatment and also a short interview with another man who had complained against the police. In return I could have the full hour of

Tonight, which could include up to 40 minutes of my interview of O'Connor. When I returned to Enniskillen I found the nationalist community confirmed in its suspicion that the BBC would never be allowed (or, perhaps, want) to put out this programme. The credibility of the BBC's claim to be impartial as between the two communities was visibly at stake.

In the event, the RUC declined to comment except for a one line statement, to which we, of course, give full prominence. I had been asked to make an introductory statement – I used this to emphasise the grave nature of the security situation and the perilous task of the RUC, but I also laid out the facts of the European Commission's finding and the Attorney-General's speech.

All hell broke loose the following day; the BBC was under intense attack in the tabloids, the cartoonists had a field day, one ('Jak' in the *Evening Standard*) showing a man spreadeagled on the pavement and a BBC reporter, not, I was glad to note, looking particularly like me, offering a microphone to masked gunmen, bristling with machine-guns and inviting their opinion. Even *The Times*, in a leader which generally rebutted the wider criticisms of the BBC's coverage of Northern Ireland, defined the issues raised by the O'Connor interviews very fairly, only to come down on balance against the showing of it. The day afterwards was to be the regular meeting of the BBC Board of Governors and, at the Director-General's request, Ms Thomason and I stayed up all night preparing a detailed report on every stage of our actions. Fortunately the Governors backed without reservation the decision to transmit.

Reactions in the Province can be guessed: favourable comment in the *Irish News* and by civil rights activists and the SDLP; bitter resentment by spokesmen of the Unionists and the RUC. The Vanguard Unionist party expressed its 'utter revulsion' at the programme and went on, 'Amazement is the only description one can give to the fantastic memory of the alleged victim, who despite his terrible suffering was able to memorise every single event including the actual length of each happening. How gullible does the BBC think the public are?' An RUC spokesman was quoted in the press as saying that, 'The fear here is that terrorists might seize on this as provocation to kill more policemen.'

At the time of the O'Connor interview 99 Ulster police had been murdered since the Provo violence had begun. Eleven days after the interview, 18 year old Police Constable William Brown was killed by the IRA in Fermanagh: the Provos' statement sought to link this with the RUC having been 'shown to the world as the torture instrument of the British war machine.' This translated into a banner headline, 'MURDER BY TV; BBC accused after assassination' on the front page of the *Daily Express*. The chairman of the Ulster Police Federation was quoted as saying that the *Tonight* programme had borne the hallmarks of trial by TV. In the House of Lords, Viscount Brookborough, son of the late Prime Minster of Northern Ireland, demanded to know 'At what stage does a part of the State establishment provide the IRA with a platform on which to put their view?' The BBC kept cool under the pressure; the Director-General, Sir Charles Curran, said that the IRA needed no fresh excuse for killing members of the security forces.

The Attorney-General sent for me. He had read the script of the film and was in obvious distress at the apparent breach of his pledge to the Council of Europe. There was an official procedure for complaints against the police and O'Connor had filed such a complaint. As with many previous cases the Director of Public Prosecutions had decided that there was insufficient evidence for action to be taken against the police officers at Castlereagh. But the Attorney-General took pains to explain to me the advantages to a person in O'Connor's position of going to court with a civil suit against the Chief Constable of the RUC, since the standards of proof required of the plaintiff are not so exacting as those required for a criminal prosecution – 'beyond reasonable doubt' for the latter but only 'balance of probabilities' in a civil case. Silkin did this in a way which made me feel that he was as good as offering his legal advice to O'Connor to press the suit. O'Connor was in any case inclined to sue.

I was extremely interested in the result. I had done my best to test O'Connor's *bona fides* but I am not a lawyer and this was the first time he would be publicly examined by lawyers. The legal process known as 'discovery' revealed the identities and time cards of O'Connor's various interrogators, showing the extraordinary accuracy of his account on television. Some of his allegations of the application of violence were thought by Mr Justice Murray to be exaggerated. Notwithstanding this, on 30 June 1980, more than three years after his ordeal, Bernard O'Connor was awarded exemplary damages.[4]

It should not be thought that every one of the many reports from Ireland which I made at various intervals throughout the Seventies up until my *Two Traditions in Ireland* in 1980 were occasions for controversy. Quite the contrary in fact, they usually were not. I have simply picked out instances which may cast some light on the issues confronting the media when disorder strikes close to home.

In personal terms, I was suddenly recognised wherever I went. I was a celebrity at GAA fixtures! Hard line Protestants wanted me burned; moderate Protestants sympathised with me; I won huge respect in Nationalist circles. But the psychological impact of my interrogation and torture was evidencing itself. I was off school for three months, and undoubtedly returned far too soon. My moods drove me crazy. I was terrified of being shot by the UVF, as predicted by my interrogators. I did see a psychiatrist, but these were different times before the legacy of trauma was diagnosed, recognised or treated. I was given mind-numbing medication which I stopped taking the day I missed three steps coming downstairs and hit my head on the wall. I took to varying my movements, out of fear, including sleeping away from home.

In one of the worst moves of my life, we decided to buy a pub in Ballyfarnon in Roscommon – back to my roots in the licensed trade, though we employed staff to run it and I continued teaching. My wife Pat and the children went there to live, and I divided my time between there and Willoughby Place, which we kept on, with the children being driven to and from school in Enniskillen every day. It was crazy. I had undergone such a huge change of character. I was so angry. I lost my temper so easily. I certainly should not have been teaching. And still, when I was in Enniskillen, the threatening phone calls continued, at three and four in the morning. Long, heavy breathing. The sound of a clock ticking as surely as it was ticking for me. I reported them, to no avail. I was constantly stopped and harassed by the police at every possible opportunity. Knowledge of my civil case was becoming widespread.

Every possible legal tactic was used to try to prevent or delay it coming to court. Police witnesses were unavailable. So were documents. I was only granted partial legal aid so, if my case was unsuccessful, I faced financial ruin. It eventually reached court three years after I instigated proceedings, in 1980. By now, we had sold the pub and the family was back in Willoughby Place with the addition of our eighth and final child, baby Meabh.

The first attempt at proceedings lasted only four days. The case was to be heard by the Lord Chief Justice, Lord Lowry. In a bizarre turn of fate, it emerged that one of the Special Branch officers who had brutally interrogated me, and was a key witness, had begun a relationship with Lord Lowry's daughter who was now pregnant. It was suggested to Tony McGettigan that this might be prejudicial to the case, and perhaps he should ask for Lord Lowry to be removed? My solicitor was too wise for this, replying simply that he was quite sure such a senior figure as the Lord Chief Justice was above prejudice. Lord Lowry withdrew, and Mr Justice Murray replaced him.

By now, we had amassed additional evidence in support of my case. Fathers Denis Faul and Raymond Murray, who had written and published widely on torture in Castlereagh, took an interest in my case and arranged for a doctor from Amnesty to examine me in the Europa Hotel in Belfast. He discovered a lesion on the right-hand side of my brain. The Amnesty report carried great weight and put my case on an international platform. It added further gravitas to the evidence with which myself, Tony McGettigan, junior QC James Brady and senior QC Charles Hill entered the courtroom in Chichester Street. I had been granted leave of absence from work.

From the outset, there was huge interest in the case among the legal profession. Many barristers not involved in the case would attend regularly to see what they knew was history being made. The atmosphere was bustling and highly charged. The public could not know this at the time however, as the government had served a D notice on the proceedings, banning media coverage. Michael Breslin of my local paper, the *Fermanagh Herald*, did try to attend on one occasion but was turned away. There was one solitary "reporter" in court whose identity I never knew. Suffice to say, when I was giving evidence, every word was issued to the media. When the 38 detectives were cross-examined and shown to perjure themselves time and again, not a word appeared. I, of course, was effectively gagged as everything was sub judice.

The first disputes were over the admissibility of documents, and in the end all the evidential papers we wished to be considered, from the Amnesty report to the detectives' time sheets, were admitted. One dispute which arose was over whether the Secretary of State Roy Mason had signed the papers extending my detention period. It emerged that he hadn't – the papers had simply been signed by a civil servant. The fact that the police objections to the admission of documents were overruled was to change the pattern of the whole case.

I was first into the witness box and over the course of four days I was cross-examined by the police's QC, Mr Campbell. He used many tactics that were all too familiar to me from Castlereagh; he tried to confuse me, and I was constantly challenged.

My own GP Dr Mulhern gave evidence on my behalf, listing the injuries he had seen and reported when he visited me in Castlereagh. His testimony was convincing; he was impressively measured, calm and conservative in his demeanour. When the police called their doctor, Dr Dean, my senior QC challenged him on every word of his denial of seeing evidence of my injuries until he conceded that he "might" and "maybe did" see them. A victory for us.

Brother Peter, my school principal, also gave evidence, testifying to the condition he had found me in when he visited my home the day after my release. He, too, had seen the injuries.

At this point another example of the sinister and devious tactics used at Castlereagh became clear to me. The shower I had been offered, when the water was inexplicably freezing cold though the central heating was on full blast, had not been a kind gesture to freshen me up; it had been a tactical move to minimise the bruising and swelling to my face and body. How little I had known.

38 detectives were called to the stand and my senior QC, Charles Hill, was relentless and ruthless in challenging every detail. The detectives' time sheets, which the court had ruled must be disclosed, soon gave lie to their statements that I had been given adequate breaks, rest and sleep between interrogations and proved my evidence that I had been sleep deprived and questioned for hours without a break. Quite clearly, they were giving false testimony. We recorded two other major successes.

The police witnesses had tried to refute my evidence about the waste paper bin being emptied over my head so that I had to pick up the rubbish like an animal with my mouth, by insisting they used envelope type bins. One by one they insisted this. Then finally one detective, who clearly had not attended their briefing, was encouraged by Charles Hill to tell the court what he would have done if I had signed a statement and later retracted it. The detective said without hesitation that he would have torn it up and thrown it in the bin (a lie in itself) and happily agreed that the bins in Castlereagh were identical to those in the court. Conventional, bucket bins. The judge produced one from below his bench. Yes, the detective agreed, just like that. Even Chief Inspector Caskey had sworn they only had envelope type bins.

One of the most vicious detectives, the one who had spun me over his head and thrown me across the room so I landed on my back, had never appeared in court. I had given a detailed description of him, the police response being that no such person existed. On the second last day of the hearing, he appeared and sat on the end of the seat with the other detectives. I passed a note to my solicitor who briefed Mr Hill, who secured an immediate intervention. I was asked to pick him out. The judge ordered him to stand. He clearly matched my description in every detail. The detectives' time sheets proved that Detective Sergeant Taylor was indeed on duty that night in that cell block. It became known as the "Campbell Taylor Test," the judge would refer to it more than once. And I had passed it.

25

THE JUDGMENT – LORD JUSTICE MURRAY 30TH JUNE 1980

Justice Murray gave a long and detailed judgment, some 87 pages in length. He began by outlining my background as a teacher, Scout leader, community worker and civil rights activist. He went on to go through my arrest in detail, early detention, interrogations, my release without charge and subsequent claims that I was making. He particularly referred to the humane kindness of Inspector Curry for having offered to drive me home and avoid my wife having to drive from Enniskillen to collect me after her caesarean operation a few days earlier.

He paid particular attention to the timeline regarding my release, my immediate statement of abuse to my solicitor, the prompt interview with the two senior officers, Superintendent Hood and Inspector Brown, within days, and my TV appearance, all showing detailed consistency. He stated, "His memory for detail was remarkably accurate. Finally, in the first week of March 1977, he took the quite extraordinary step of appearing on television and telling the public the story of his ill treatment in Castlereagh."

He then analysed the different medical reports of the four doctors I met in Castlereagh, the two Danish doctors I met in the Europa Hotel, Belfast, through Amnesty, my psychiatrist, Mr Egan and the other police specialists that I had to appear before after my time in Castlereagh. The two Danish doctors diagnosed me as having "cerebral asthenopia" which is brain damage from abuse.

The judge went on to list 11 areas where he claimed my outstanding counsel – Mr Charles Hill, Senior Counsel and Junior Counsel James Brady – were claiming as infringements of my civil rights and where torture and inhumane treatment had taken place. These included wrongful arrest, excessive detention, assault and battery, excessive length of interrogations, sleep deprivation, no access to mental and physical recreation, torture, both physical and mental, degrading verbal abuse, religious abuse, white light treatment, stripping, sexually explicit comments, fear, exhausting activities, all-night mental abuse, hooding, suffocation, false acts of kindness and denial of access to legal help.

The medical evidence was a significant factor in proving some of the above. The Judge said, "I now turn to the medical evidence which, in my view, is of crucial importance in the case. It is the evidence of Dr Felix Mulhern, the plaintiff's own family doctor."

He quoted Dr Mulhern's evidence: "'Generally sweaty and face unshaven. Not particularly untidy. Removed his clothing; very slow in taking off his jumper and shirt. Told me he had great pain as he had had to stand in a squatting position with his hands outstretched. Undressing difficulty probably caused by some degree of muscle soreness. Examined his head. Two very obvious injuries to ears; right ear and left; blueish black colour; left somewhat deeper colour. Only part of the ears not appearing to be bruised were the lobes. Bruising under the left eye; half an inch – 1 inch to cheekbone on the left. Bruising of upper anterior chest wall 2 – 3 inches across. Not as deep a blue as the ear injuries – lighter blue. All fairly fresh bruises, within last three days. Left eye bruise approx. same age. Ears fresh bruises too. Told me he had been punched in the back of the neck. I examined his cervical spine. Found when I asked him to flex his neck and shoulders that his movement was a lot slower than one would expect. This indicated some form of muscular injury – muscles tense. What I found confirmed what he told me. I examined the kidney area, left and right. Found tenderness. Legs – no bruises.'"

The Judge referred to Dr Mulhern's second examination of me at my home the day after my release and noted his similar findings as well as my need for treatment for depression and anxiety. This evidence was further supported by Dr Mulhern's partner, Dr Brennan, who examined me on 27th January, and then by the psychiatrist, Mr Egan, who all concurred.

The Judge could not understand why or how Dr Dean, the police doctor, had not seen the injuries on me when Dr Mulhern was examining me. However, under cross-examination by Mr Hill, my QC, the judge noted Dr Dean's responses: "'I accept Dr Mulhern found bruises on ears; possibly O'Connor had bruises, I did not see. I would say "yes" he was alleging ill-treatment and would say the findings were consistent with his allegations, I accept that O'Connor had pain in his neck... complained of pain in both ears and in the epigastric region. I am satisfied that where he complained of pain he appeared to be tender... calves, lower abdomen, kidney regions'."

When it came to the evidence of the two Danish doctors from Amnesty International, the judge went to great lengths to challenge their evidence. He began by doubting their credibility, as they came from Amnesty International and were predisposed to contradicting the authorities. He disputed the methods and tests they used to come to their diagnosis. He was not convinced and therefore ruled out their findings.

In relation to my evidence versus that of the police, especially the Chief Superintendent, and despite having complimented me for having an amazing memory, the Judge concluded that I was not truthful, made false allegations and exaggerated on a number of occasions. I stated that I distinctly heard other people being abused by detectives in other rooms in the interrogation centre in my submission. The Judge dismissed this as "having a distinctly false ring about it." Yet he referred my statements to my solicitor, the Complaints and Discipline team and the TV programme as consistent and prompt. He claimed that my TV appearance was politically motivated rather than, as my QC Mr Hill stressed, "To expose ill-treatment, torture and a denial of basic human and civil rights."

It confirmed to me what the Chief Superintendent had said to me during an interrogation session: "When we go into court and make false allegations, the judge will believe us."

Yet the Judge in another part of his judgment showed more inconsistency when he stated, "Since the plaintiff was not charged with any offence, he had no need or motive to make false complaints of ill treatment to save himself from conviction on grave terrorist charges as many terrorists have undoubtedly done in the criminal courts of this country in recent years."

Referring to when the police were tripped up in their evidence in the witness box by my QC – for example with the waste paper bin evidence, the clock issue in the cell block and the Campbell Taylor test – he dismissed these as not significant. Added to this was the failure of the Judge to accept that system in Castlereagh was well orchestrated, meticulously designed for torture techniques, psychological disorientation of the mind (brainwashing) and the breaking of the suspect. Evidence of this was the declaration by every one of the 38 detectives under cross-examination that they all had been trained in interrogation techniques at Sandhurst in England. The Judge suggested that, "Having heard from the Chief Superintendent and the other detectives involved a complete denial that they were instructed to or did use any kind of system of interrogation against the plaintiff, and having reviewed all the evidence, I reject Mr Hill's submission. It is clear that different detectives use different methods – just as different forensic cross-examiners use different techniques with witnesses."

The Judge failed to hear several detectives under cross-examination refer to several briefing sessions both before my interrogations and during my five days in Castlereagh. Even the two interrogators who had me for six hours until 5 a.m. on Sunday morning, and who referred to themselves as "the night shift workers," both explained in detail that they were instructed by the Chief Superintendent to, "keep him talking as long as possible." The reason of course why this tactic was adopted was clear. The night before, when I was interrogated until after 2 a.m., they saw that I was becoming disorientated and brainwashed, so they expected the same to happen again.

In relation to this particular interview and those prior to it, the Judge stated the following, "... apart from those two breaks it is accepted by the defence that starting at 10.30

a.m. on the Saturday the plaintiff was interviewed through the night. Had the investigation reached a critical point by, say, midnight when N and F could reasonably say that to break off for the night would have hindered or delayed the process of investigation? In my view this could not be said."

The Judge continued to say, "I have, accordingly, reached the conclusion that in the circumstances I have described in relation to this interview – and I emphasise these words – that the use of the police questioning power by F and N was excessive and unjustified. The plaintiff said that this long interview caused him grave mental distress and the defence accepted that there was evidence of the plaintiff being disorientated in relation to the events of the Sunday morning following the F/N interview."

However, the Judge did find that two of the six interrogators who physically abused me were guilty of physically abusing me, although he referred to my injuries as "not serious or lasting." He stated that: "The main effect of the ill-treatment and the excessively long interrogations of the plaintiff was mental. I have been asked to consider exemplary damages and I take the view that this case is a proper one for such an award."

Thanks to the tireless and thorough work put into this case by my solicitor, Tony McGettigan, and his secretary Mrs Eleanor Morris, as well as the guidance, direction and outstanding courtroom skills of my QC Charles Hill and his assistant James Brady who exposed the brutal police system of interrogation in Castlereagh, we had, for the first time, won a case against them.

Recently, 40 years after the case, Tony McGettigan met a granddaughter of mine in a pharmacy in Enniskillen. On discovering that I was her grandfather, he told her, "Your Grandfather and I made history in Northern Ireland. We were the first to ever win a case of torture against the RUC."

And that is our enduring legacy.

26

LIFE CHANGING REPERCUSSIONS

We had won the case, but at a huge personal cost. Emotions in our home were on a permanent rollercoaster. There were constant threatening phone calls during the night. An incendiary device was put through our letter box. It turned out to be a hoax, but we weren't to know it at the time. A schoolboy from Portora threw a brick through our window. I intervened to prevent his expulsion. I was sitting in my parked car in town, chatting to an acquaintance through the window, when a Loyalist came up and punched me in the face. He was convicted of assault. I had a good rapport with the newly appointed Chief Superintendent Glasgow in Enniskillen RUC station, who advised me on personal security, informing me he was "aware of threats on my life." We had a peep hole fitted in the front door and checking underneath the car before driving off became a way of life.

Every morning, driving to school, I was aware of a police presence on the roads. There were two different sections of policing, the local patrols and the DMSU. The latter were politically motivated and the difference in attitude became clear in the all too frequent occasions when we were stopped and searched. In August 1984, for example, I was stopped and searched 24 times; another month it was 25, almost daily. The pressure was unbelievable and took its toll on the family. I couldn't rationalise things. My wife, in her distress, blamed more and more my involvement with civil rights for the harassment we faced.

On occasions, I became aware that I was being followed. Around two months before Loyalists attempted to murder me, I noticed a car acting suspiciously as I locked up the Scout Hall and handed over the keys. I asked the caretaker to ring me if this car followed me. I had driven only a short distance when he rang to confirm that it was. I diverted to the Erne Hospital, parked and walked through the building to the exit where I rang for one of the family to collect me, leaving my car in the car park. I was genuinely afraid. The next Sunday, while taking a driving lesson in the country, I noticed a car acting suspiciously, doing repeated three-point turns. Was it my imagination? Or something more sinister? I was acutely aware that during my interrogation in Castlereagh, detectives had repeatedly threatened that my details would be passed on to Loyalist paramilitaries, specifically the UVF, and that if I walked free from questioning, I was as good as dead. It was only a matter of where and when.

The next Sunday, in April 1983, we went to half past 10 Mass at the Graan, celebrated as always by Father Brian D'Arcy. He referred to the fact that Armagh were playing Down in the National League final at Croke Park that afternoon. My wife was a lifelong Down supporter and on the spur of the moment, I decided to go to Dublin, dropping off the children with my Uncle Benny's family in Dublin. He was the same uncle who had carried me into Croke Park on his shoulders in 1957. I cancelled a scheduled driving lesson in Enniskillen with a regular pupil, a young man who worked at Belleek Pottery, and off we went.

But the Loyalist gunmen who set out to kill me during that lesson did not know this. Instead, when I did not turn up where they expected, they spent the afternoon looking for me around hotels in the town. They had my details in their pocket. At around eight o'clock that evening, deprived of their intended victim, they shot dead a young Catholic man walking home from the town. By chance, he was shot outside a UDR soldier's house. The alarm was raised and the police, thinking the UDR man had been attacked, were on the scene within minutes and the gunmen were arrested.

Sadly, and ironically, the young man they murdered, who had been in the wrong place at the wrong time, was one of my former pupils. But we, on our spontaneous day out, were oblivious to this.

On our way home, at around midnight, we were stopped at Butlersbridge. Referring to me by name, a soldier told me to "wait a while there" and immediately the bollards came up, closing the road. After around 10 minutes, a police car arrived. The bollards were put down and we were ordered to follow the police car. I was very scared. I was sure I was being arrested and taken back to Castlereagh. As we passed Lisnaskea RUC station the car pulled in, we were waved on and another police car drove ahead of us all the way to our front door, parking across the road with all its doors open. We carried the sleeping children into the house and put them to bed. The car drove off. I couldn't understand this.

The next morning, I tuned in to the eight o'clock local news on the radio, something I did every morning, to hear that a young man had been shot dead in Enniskillen the previous afternoon. School was closed for the Easter holidays and at half past nine, two plain-clothes police officers arrived at the house to warn me, as I had already been warned, that my life was in danger. Only when Superintendent Glasgow arrived an hour later did the picture become clear. He told me that the murder of the day before had begun as an attempt to shoot me.

I attended the trial of my would-be assassins, Robert James Kenny and Mark Trotter, on 8th September that year. They were charged with the murder of the young man, and my attempted murder. It was disclosed that both were serving members of the security forces and that the gun they used was a police issue revolver belonging to a relative of one of them. At the last minute they pleaded guilty, so no further details of collusion were made public. They were given life sentences.

The harassment of myself and my family continued. Our phone was tapped. Nowhere was this more evident than when we were discussing arrangements for my wife's sister's funeral. We were detained for an hour on the way there and missed it, which was deeply traumatic for Pat and did nothing to lessen the tension between us. Our marriage had deteriorated into constant rows. When Aine fell off her skateboard, developed a hip infection and was transferred from the Erne hospital to Musgrave Park in Belfast, Pat stayed in Belfast for the six weeks that Aine was there. I drove up and down every day after school. We were both mentally and physically exhausted and this became, "another sign of the bad luck you have brought on us." We and the children were the collateral damage of Castlereagh and all that ensued thereafter. The intensity and regularity of the harassment and intimidation caused us to focus on survival and, as a result, we failed to recognise the emotional and psychological damage that was happening to both ourselves and, in particular, our children. In the circumstances, Pat proved to be a wonderful mother. Together we did our best to provide a good home, resourcefully, nutritionally, spiritually and educationally for all of the children, but not realising the psychological damage and trauma that was inflicted on us and them.

I tried to hang on to my sanity by immersing myself in

the Scouts, and by successfully completing a Master's in Education. It was displacement activity, a distraction. I had returned to school after three months off. In retrospect, it should have been three years. I was too angry and intolerant of the children. But I was stubborn, determined not to let the police feel they had won. The school needed me, and I felt I needed the normality. But it was far from normality: we were on our knees.

I used part of the all-too-small court compensation to buy a Mazda car. Stopped, as was usual, by the police, an officer asked me whether every single part of the car was Japanese. My riposte was: "You should know, you bought it for me!"

He went berserk. I left the car and walked to the police station to make a complaint. The officer involved would later make a formal apology to me at my home. Meanwhile, my wife, driving past, saw my abandoned car and assumed I'd been arrested. Her outburst to the police got her arrested, until the situation calmed down.

The harassment continued. Taking a television for repair, I was made to take it apart to prove I wasn't concealing guns or ammunition inside. Coming up to Christmas, the Scout band always played carols in the town centre. That year, I had to collect and return our young tuba player from Gortatole, where he was on an outward-bound course. On my way back I was detained by DMSU personnel, whose harassment included opening up all our instruments and going through some 300 pages of sheet music to see if there was writing on them, then letting them scatter in the wind. By chance, the Commissioner of the Baden Powell Scouts, Mark Scott, with whom I had good relations, happened to drive past and stopped to see what was going on. He helped to sort things out and later made a formal complaint on my behalf.

In 1987, I was offered another fresh start when I was appointed principal of St Patrick's, a small rural school at Mullanaskea, three miles outside Enniskillen. It was a huge challenge as it was in a terrible state, with just 77 pupils on roll. I absorbed myself in it – I lived, ate and slept there – coming home only briefly after class for my dinner and going straight back, working until 11 or 12 at night. In 10 years I would completely turn round its fortunes. But it was also an avoidance technique to keep me away from the deteriorating situation at home. Three children had gone to university, Nuala had entered a convent and a fifth had gone to America. Rows between Pat and myself were the norm. At this time the Scout band had a major US tour – another great success but another avoidance technique and distraction for me. Anything to escape life at home.

Pat considered and made moves to leave a few times in 1987 and '88 but it was a further, seismic destruction of family life that in the end proved the catalyst. One Saturday in April 1989, our 12-year-old daughter was stopped by three police officers, pulled into the back of their car and sexually assaulted. We knew nothing until the Monday when her principal rang to tell us she had been admitted to the Erne hospital. She had bought a box of paracetamol on the way to school, taken them, then told her form teacher what she had done and why. We rushed to her bedside where she was unconscious after her stomach had been pumped. We were beyond devastated.

Mercifully, she recovered physically but, back home, her condition deteriorated. She made an official complaint to the police as to her alleged abusers but was afraid to carry it through because her alleged abusers told her I would be shot if she did. She was not prepared to risk that. We found that this threat was being perpetrated in telephone calls to our home and that she was also threatened that if she pursued a complaint, her younger sister would be sexually abused. Then further disclosures: her two elder sisters still at home confided the same thing had happened to them. They made statements but would take it no further.

Thanks to the intervention of the Chief Scout in Dublin, Paul Ring, a meeting was arranged with representatives of the Department of Foreign Affairs in Dublin. They raised the matter with the British government and as a result Superintendent John Middlemas of the London Metropolitan Police was sent to Enniskillen to investigate. He met me weekly at school to report on his progress. I found him pleasant and cooperative and so cooperated in turn, despite my own experiences of police investigations.

After three months, he told me he had identified the suspects. They had stonewalled his questioning, but their time sheets put them in the right place and time for the alleged assaults. To proceed further, my daughters would have to agree to attend an identity parade and pick out their attackers. Because of the threat to my life, they declined. However, I did note his observation that one of the accused had a physical deformity – a deformity that exactly matched that of one of my most brutal interrogators in Castlereagh.

As a result of his investigation, all my daughters, including the 10-year-old, were issued with rape alarms to carry everywhere, day and night. The youngest has worn hers everywhere life has taken her, and she still has it to this day.

Pat left in 1993. By then only the youngest remained at home and she stayed with me in the family house. When she went to college four years later, I kept the light on and the radio playing in her bedroom to ensure some sort of presence. I was in a bad way. In truth, I was suicidal.

It was a friend from Scouts, Gerry Moan, who saved me. Calling at the house, we started talking and he grasped the enormity of the situation. Then he said the words that would change my life: "I know someone who can help you."

That "someone" was his friend Mrs Neville, a psychotherapist based in Dublin. I drove up and down every week to see her. For the first few months, I just sat and cried tears that had been suppressed for 20 years. Then I began to talk. It was the start of my healing. The Scouts and the school had enabled me to survive, but now I was starting to recover.

The school was thriving. In 10 years, the number on roll had gone from 77 to 200. From a school with little academic reputation, we were recording an 80 to 90% success rate in the 11 Plus exam. We were winning trophies for football, swimming and hurling. We organised concerts and fundraisers and the community was thrilled with the sense of pride and involvement. Every year we recruited another teacher and expanded into another classroom. One new appointment was a young man who had done his teaching practice with me. Energetic and sports-focussed, he was popular with staff and pupils alike. I was delighted.

One Monday morning, three years later, he didn't turn up for work. I was told he was unwell. Shortly afterwards, a police Chief Superintendent arrived at the office and asked to speak to me in private. His opening words shocked me: "I'm sure you know we arrested one of your members of staff this morning." I explained that I didn't. What was the charge? "Child abuse." I immediately thought he meant the teacher had hit a child and there had been a complaint. No, the Chief Super explained, "sexual abuse."

I nearly fell off the chair. My legs buckled under me.

"Wee girls?" I asked.

"Wee boys." And I was told the police had grade A evidence implicating him.

I was stunned. I was asked not to tell the other staff for

now and advised a forensic team would arrive shortly to examine the portable classroom where the man had taught, which they did.

When they heard the news, my colleagues were similarly shocked. This bright, sporty young man, chatty and flirty with female staff, had been the perfect paedophile.

The story had broken one Sunday afternoon when a victim's uncle had taken him to the beach and noticed the inappropriate way the boy was playing with and holding his cousins. He told his uncle that, "that's the way the teacher catches the boys in school." He then went on to innocently describe behaviour that was clearly abusive. His uncle took him to the police station where they lodged a formal complaint. During interview, the boy identified many other pupils who had been abused the same way. The boy was kept off school on the Monday and that evening, social workers and police called at the home of all the boys he had identified to interview them and take statements. These boys in turn were kept off school the next day. In hindsight, I had noticed this, as our attendance record was excellent. Over the coming weeks, the police would go through school records with me, identifying pupils who had been taught over the three years the accused had been in the school. They were then interviewed. In all, 40 boys would make complaints of abuse, and 25 would proceed to court. The teacher pleaded guilty and was sentenced to three years in jail.

He was released after 18 months.

Not one of his victims had confided in a parent or a teacher. Every one of them described him as "the best teacher they ever had." Such is the power of grooming. It broke me completely.

I was off school for six months. The day I came back, I was walking down the corridor past the toilets when a Primary One pupil accosted me, looking for assistance: "Master, my zip is stuck." I couldn't help him. School life was forever changed by the necessary enforcement of a vast amount of child and teacher protection. We already had good safeguarding policies in place. Now, there were more restrictions. No more giving pupil's lifts, no more combing hair or towelling dry after swimming when the bus was ready to leave. Restrictions and restraints – necessary though they were – affecting every aspect of school life.

My one comfort and motivation to continue was that not one family took their child away from the school as a result.

11th October 1984

Chief Constable,
R.U.C.,
"Brooklyn",
Knock Road,
Belfast.

Dear Sir,

Bernard O'Connor - Complaint

We act for Mr. Bernard O'Connor of 38 Willoughby Place, Enniskillen, Co. Fermanagh.

We are instructed by our client that since the 20th August 1984 he and his wife and family have been involved in at least 24 incidents involving members of the D.M.S.U. stationed at St. Angelo, Enniskillen.

Of these 24 incidents 15 relate to Mr. O'Connor and/or his wife being stopped at vehicle check points set up by the D.M.S.U. at which Mr. O'Connor and/or his family were subjected to detailed personal searches and close interrogations and in which their vehicles had been very thoroughly searched.

It would appear that other vehicles and other persons passing through these vehicle check points were not subjected to the same close and detailed searches and interrogations.

The remaining 9 incidents relate to vehicle check points being set up close to Mr. O'Connor's home and during the course of the time when the V.C.P.'s were in operation Mr. O'Connor and/or his wife and children were subjected to attention from the members of the D.M.S.U. e.g. waving and shining of torch lights through the windows of their house.

The members of the R.U.C. operating these V.C.P.'s did not behave to other people in the vicinity in the same manner as they behaved towards the O'Connor family and household.

Mr. O'Connor also complains that on the morning of the 3rd October 1984 he received two obscene telephone calls in which four men took part and in which these men threaten Mr. O'Connor's life.

The four men had accents from different parts of Northern Ireland. The diverse nature of the accents leads Mr. O'Connor to believe that there is a possibility that they were members of the Police force - a suspicion which was greatly re-enforced by the fact that the persons made remarks which indicated that they had access to information which only the Police would have or should have had access to.

Mr. O'Connor and his family take these threats to his life very seriously indeed and he is also perturbed by the behaviour of the Police at the vehicle check points and at his home. Mr. O'Connor is a law abiding citizen and no cause or justification exists for the incidents complained of although the telephone calls are separate from and much more serious than the other incidents involving the D.M.S.U. which are merely oppressive and intimidating.

In these circumstances we should be glad if you would treat this letter as a formal complaint and arrange to have the behaviour of the Police concerned investigated as a matter of urgency.

Yours faithfully,
P.J. FLANAGAN & CO.

PER ....

C.C.
Chief Superintendent, R.U.C., Enniskillen and
Police Authority for Northern Ireland, River House, High Street, Belfast.

Castlereagh in East Belfast, Strand Road in Derry and Gough Barracks in Armagh. Arguably the most notable was Enniskillen head teacher, Bernard O'Connor whose ill-treatment at the hands of Special Branch interrogators

killed me and very nearly did at one stage of the interrogation. The idea was to get you to make statements for them to stop it."

In the course of one three-year period, more than 3,000 people were

told Roy Mason that the legal profession, 'shared the conviction that ill-treatment of suspects by police officers with the object of obtaining confessions is now common practice'.

The letter highlighted Castlereagh

Dr W. Baird wrote to the Chief Constable.

He told Sir Kenneth Newman that the Police Authority had met three Police doctors (they were on duty at holding centres) who were worried about a

his transfer request. In March the following year, the Bennett Report confirmed medical evidence of ill-treatment and the UK government accepted its main recommendations, including cctv.

O'Connor abuse case led to reform

Retired Enniskillen headmaster, Bernard O'Connor, a long time local Scout leader, won't ever forget his introduction to a five-day detention in Castlereagh Holding Centre, and to the first of his Special Branch interrogators.

Over the course of those five days, he was questioned by 38 detectives about his alleged involvement in IRA activities back in Fermanagh.

"There was no let-up. I remember a Thursday night, it was 5 o'clock in the morning before they put me back in my cell. It was harrowing stuff."

It started as soon as he arrived in Castlereagh, having been arrested that morning, 20th January, 1977 at his home in Enniskillen: "My first introduction to the Goon Squad was an amazing one. This man who was 6' 4" with an Antrim accent took a look at me. He had a folder under his arm, he put it down on the table and he said, 'Bernard O'Connor, man but you are an insignificant little b**tard. He then drew out and hit me a box on the face. That was the start."

A Police doctor was available to detainees if they wished to make a complaint, but the Catch 22 was making matters worse for themselves if they did so.

So, Bernard O'Connor asked for his own doctor, Dr Felix Mulhern to examine him for signs of physical abuse.

His testimony was to prove crucial when he took a case against the then Secretary of State, Roy Mason and the then Chief Constable, Kenneth Newman, and won.

"When Dr Mulhern came to see me, they brought in the Police doctor with him and in the subsequent court case this Police doctor denied he saw any injuries on me whereas Dr Mulhern did. He was able to give evidence of a lot of bruises and a lot of injuries.'

The case brought by Mr O'Connor was heard in a Diplock Court (the judge sitting on his own) and, going by previous rulings, he had little chance of winning. In fact, his barrister, Charles Hill did ask him why he thought his case would be any different.

"I said to him, the only thing that would win it for me was to tell the truth, so the truth challenged the system and won out."

Mr Hill was no mug and, it was during cross-examination of the Police doctor that the cracks in the defence case began appearing. Here, the witness agreed he had given Dr Mulhern 'a skeleton pad' so that the good doctor could sketch in those body parts where he saw bruising.

At the time of Bernard O'Connor's detention in 1977, Fermanagh was comparatively peaceful, unlike, say, West Tyrone. Hence, there were few

if any complaints of people arrested and brought to Enniskillen Police Station or Omagh Station which had a certain notoriety.

But, once a detainee 'went up the road', say, to Castlereagh, the gloves were off, literally.

Among Mr O'Connor's torturers were two local Special Branch men, one of whom he readily identified by a missing finger.

"He was the worst guy of all. He really abused me. I remember him in Civil Rights days. The other amazing thing that came out of that trial was that they all had done a term of preparation (in interrogation techniques) in Sandhurst."

So, how is he doing?

"You always suffer ill-effects. To put people through what they put people through. They could have killed me, and very nearly did at one stage of the interrogation. You are made to strip naked, and they then hood you and smother you. They tread very close to killing me. The idea was to get you to make statements for them to stop it.'

As a direct result of his victory in a Diplock Court and that 'Newsnight' programme, and pressure from elsewhere, the Bennett Report ushered in reforms where the rights of detainees were protected, the use of cctv, etc.

Bernard O'Connor whose abuse case led to reform. GKFH42

27

NEW BEGINNINGS

Knowing my marriage was over and my life was falling apart, despite the outward display of a competent, brave and enthusiastic public face to the staff and parents at the school and Scouting community, I found myself trying to make relationships work with other females. My personal problems, and failure to recognise them, were making me more and more incompatible to others and led me into mistake after mistake. Having exited from a rollercoaster relationship of almost seven years, I decided to rebuild myself. I did a degree course in Personal-Centered Counselling with the UUJ, which helped me to deal with parental, pupil and personal issues in my role as a school principal and as a Scout Commissioner, especially after the sexual abuse scandal which hit our school. However, worse was to come.

A four-year-old P1 pupil, while playing in the playground during lunch break, was shot in the head. At first it was thought that the child fell in the playground and hit his head off the kerb. The child had a small cut to the back of its head, and it was bleeding slightly. He was fully conscious. In keeping with school policy, all such casualties are immediately brought to the local Erne Hospital. We were completely shocked when the police arrived at the school to inform us that the child had a bullet lodged in its brain. A bullet had entered the child's head from the rear and was lodged behind the child's forehead bone. The child was rushed to the Royal Victoria Hospital, Belfast, where after two very intense and skilled operations by a team of surgeons, the bullet was removed. The child regained consciousness after an agonising six weeks for all of us in the school, but especially for his parents and wider family. He went on to make a great recovery.

Intense police investigations were carried out in the area for months afterwards and it was eventually discovered that a local farmer had been pigeon shooting about a mile away and a stray bullet entered the playground.

It was just one traumatic event after another. It brought to a head the realisation that I needed to adopt a support mechanism to be able to cope, so I began to focus on myself. Some amazing events happened over these traumatic years which gave me encouragement. In recognition for the way we dealt with the shooting incident at the school, our success in building a new school and the achievements of the school, I was invited to a special awards evening by Prime Minister Tony Blair and his wife at 10 Downing Street. In Scouting,

I was awarded the Silver Wolfhound, which is the highest award one can get. Myself and the Scout Band were given a special award by Prince Charles and the Prince's Trust. In New York, Mayor Guliani awarded the Scout Band the Freedom of the City and I was given the US Army's Medallion of Honour by their Commander, Col. Tracey Nicolson in Fort Hamilton for my outstanding services to Scouting. The band and I were recognised by the late and great Danny Murphy, Ulster Council GAA, who presented me with a plaque of recognition for my and the band's services to Ulster GAA.

Despite these and many more successful events and moments, the euphoria would not last. I was now in the twilight of my teaching career and facing retirement in a few years. I had been in the teaching profession for 38 years, so it was time to really focus on a new way forward. I had faced so much trauma: the events of Castlereagh, the murder attempt, the sexual abuse of the girls, the marriage break-up, the constant pressure and fear on the rest of the family, the sexual abuse of the children in the school by a male teacher, another broken relationship, the child having been shot in the school playground. Without doubt, I had been the victim of layers of Post-Traumatic Stress Disorder (PTSD). The message became very clear eventually. Counselling had been a source of strength to me in the past, as had the enormous support of Dr Mulhern and my two friends, Seamus and Gerry.

As a follow up to my Counselling qualification I received from the UUJ, I applied to DCU to do a Master's degree in counselling and psychotherapy. I successfully passed the interview and for the next three years I attended lectures in the DCU Medical Campus, qualifying in 2004. Three years later, I qualified with a diploma in psychosexual therapy. These turned out to be the best achievements of my life.

In tandem with my professional development, it was my good fortune to meet Roisin in 2001. For years, friends had been urging me to get out and about more. I was however warned in the most affectionate way about having my good friend Seamus as my "wing man" for he was legendary in his success with the opposite sex. But fate smiled upon me on my 60th birthday. I'd gone to a dance in a hotel in Newry, the Canal Court, fell into conversation with Roisin and we agreed to keep in touch. We married 11 years ago so the rest is happy history!

I was by now in a different place in my life. Because of my past terrible and traumatic experiences, I was now in a position to use all that terrible and traumatic background to help others. Irrespective of what problems others came to me with, I felt I was well equipped to have a full understanding of their feelings and be totally empathic to them. For 16 years I worked with Accord marriage counselling services, and at present I work with Counselling Connections, Dundalk, and with several medical centres on both sides of the border. I have now spent many thousands of hours in the counselling room over the past 20 years and it has been the most productive and beneficial work I have ever done in my life, and that includes my positions in teaching, Scouting and the GAA. It is a wonderful experience to now help others to overcome their difficulties in life and come out the other side as I did. The courses at DCU were outstanding and life changing and to all the lecturers in the medical and counselling campus facility, I am deeply indebted. They gave me my life back and gave me the skills to be able to do the same to others.

Two other major traumatic happenings in my life must be included here. The first concerns my daughter, Nollaig, who has never fully recovered from her alleged sexual abuse at the hands of RUC officers when she was just 12 years old. A gifted musician, Nollaig went on to study Music at Aberdeen University. Family members were regular visitors; in fact, Roisin and I had returned from one such visit just a month before she disappeared, in May 2013. That was the last any of us heard from her for more than a year. We began a social media campaign to try to find her; our Facebook page attracted more than a thousand followers. Knowing her vulnerability, we were frantic with worry.

Later, we would learn that she had travelled throughout Europe until first her passport and then her violin were stolen. The breakthrough came more than a year later when Enniskillen businessman, Nicholas Cassidy, and his wife were on holiday in Murcia in Spain. Nicholas had been in

St Michael's Scout Band with Nollaig when they were young and was aware of her disappearance. Out walking one day, he saw a young woman asleep under a tree and to his shock realised it was Nollaig. Her journey back to Ireland and to long term recuperation and support had begun. Life remains challenging for Nollaig, but we are blessed to have her back.

Tragedy had not finished with the family. On St Stephen's Day 2019, just as Roisin's family had gathered for the annual celebrations, came the dreadful news that my daughter Aine's husband Dan had been killed in a road traffic accident. She was left a widow in her thirties with four young boys. Dan was such an integral part of the family. I had taught him, and he was a member of the Scouts and the band. As a solicitor, he had done ground-breaking work in helping people who had been mis-sold mortgages. He was the person everyone in the family looked to for legal advice, and more. It was such a freak accident. He will be missed forever. Somehow, together, we have found the strength to carry on and rebuild.

As I finish this narrative, where do I find myself? Blessed to be in a wonderful marriage with Roisin who, having lived in the Republic, has embraced my past with shock but above all compassion and empathy. I'm blessed too to have eight grown up children – most of whom have followed me into the teaching profession and been very successful. They have given me 22 grandchildren and three great grandchildren, with a fourth on the way. Their mother passed away last year and I hope in this narrative I have shown what a wonderful mother she was in the toughest of circumstances. We were friends.

But I know I will never be a free man. In 1986, I was arrested and held in Gough Barracks, Armagh, on the most ridiculous of charges, for three days. My mind has blanked out that experience to this day. I do recall the detective interrogating me hanging his coat over the camera in the interview room, only briefly, but commenting, "That's what we think of the O'Connor cameras," a reference to the changes that had been introduced as a result of my civil case. The Ulster Television news led that night with a headline that did my reputation no favours. Always the insinuations that a man who had never had a charge proffered against him, had somehow eluded justice.

And I was not alone. Only I know how brainwashed, how worn down, sleep deprived, physically tortured and in pain I was in Castlereagh – how very close I was to doing a deal, to confessing to crimes I had no knowledge of. It may make you smile, but I was indeed saved by a fish supper – decent food and drink for a dehydrated man. Those hungry detectives turned things round. They gave me the strength to fight on.

But what of the others, the teenagers who had fewer resources to call upon? How many young men and women lost 20 years of their life in prison for statements they were tortured into signing? What life have they had since? I urge readers to look at the writings of Fathers Faul and Murray, and Bishop Edward Daly. I won my civil case but there were many slurs and inconsistencies, factual errors and political spins in the written judgement.

The intimidation and harassment that hounded my life was the price I paid for that ruling. Even after the Enniskillen bombing, I was questioned about taking a wheelbarrow of explosives to the area. I told the police I couldn't take a wheelbarrow round my own garden! And, still, I receive the telephone calls in the wee small hours, asking for Bernard O'Sullivan, or any clearly Irish name. I am watched.

I hope my submission to the Patten report had an impact. It was held under parliamentary privilege, so I was free to speak my truth about what had been done to me, and my daughters. Yes, there have been reforms, the RUC became the PSNI with an aspirational 40% Catholic recruitment. But I understand that their detectives are still trained in brainwashing and psyops in Sandhurst.

Many years back, I went to the cinema to see *In the Name of the Father*. Coming out, I met Father Brian D'Arcy, who said, "Bernard, throughout that film, I was thinking of you." And I realise I was one of many. The Birmingham Six, The Guildford Four, so many for whom it was enough to be an Irishman in the wrong place at the wrong time when a conviction was all that mattered to an unjust police force.

And for those, like me, who survived and indeed thrived,

the collateral damage is incalculable. Poor mental health and wellbeing, families broken, and even, in my seventies, knowing I am under surveillance.

This is my testimony, written in the hope that others will understand, and that such evil injustice can never again be perpetrated on another innocent man.

HERALD

CCTV cameras proposed for Enniskillen town centre's night-time crime problem
- Page 7

tell us what you think of us and be in with the chance of winning £250 cash
- Page 22

No. 5,000 Registered as a Newspaper at the Post Office | **Wednesday, April 27th, 2005** | Price 75p (€1.20 in Republic of Ireland)

DARRAGH FIGHTING FOR HIS LIFE

5-year-old schoolboy critical as police still treat shooting as accidental

BY MICHAEL BRESLIN

The head of the Police enquiry into a shooting incident at Mullanaskea Primary School near Enniskillen on Friday afternoon has said he is still confining his enquiry to the vicinity of the school.

Five year old Darragh Somers was left in a critical state after being struck in the head by a bullet from a .22 rifle while playing in the school yard.

Yesterday his condition was described 'critical, but stable'.

Detective Chief Inspector Nigel Kyle was speaking at a media briefing at the school where he was accompanied by the school principal, Bernard O'Connor and the chairman of the school's Board of Governors, Fr John Halton, PP.

He said his particular appeal was to the person/s who might have been shooting in the vicinity of the school to give themselves up: "Someone out there knows they may be responsible for this unfortunate accident. That's the way we're looking at this at this moment in time".

However, he said he would be concerned if the person responsible had not come forward by last night (Tuesday). Pressed on that point, Mr Kyle said there could be 'something sinister' about the shooting if no one came forward.

"We have to keep an open mind in all of these things. We would not rule it out at the enquiry at some stage in the future we will have to look a wee bit wider".

The unexplained appearance at the school of a mysterious vehicle on the day of the shooting, two hours before Darragh was shot in the school playground has thrown some doubt on the 'accident' theory.

Chief Inspector Kyle explained that while two other vehicles had been eliminated from Police enquiries, this one remained unexplained: "This was a dark blue Toyota jeep which drove in through the front of the school, really turned in the playground and back out again and did not lift or leave off any kids. There doesn't seem to be any reason for it being there at all".

However, as of yesterday midday, Mr Kyle was still satisfied that the shooting

CONTINUED ON PAGE 2

Detective Chief Inspector, Nigel Kyle, second from right, talking to the media at Mullanaskea Primary School on Tuesday, where he gave details about the investigation into the shooting of Darragh Somers. Also in the photograph are, Nicola Topping Western Education and Library Board, Fr. John Halton, Parish Priest and Bernard O'Connor Principal.

Five year old Darragh Somers who was still critically ill on Tuesday.

Priest calls on gun owner to come forward

The parish priest of Tempo, Fr John Halton, who is chairman of the board of governors of St Patrick's PS, Mullanaskea yesterday made an impassioned plea to the person responsible for the accidental shooting of Darragh Somers to come forward.

And, in so doing, he echoed a message from Darragh's parents to that effect: "Darragh's father said to me: There is some man out there. He knows he has been there and he would do great favours for this community and for us all if he came forward. There has been a mistake which the Inspector has said there may well have been and, well, wouldn't it be a great uplift to us all?".

"People may have made a great mistake. We all do make mistakes and it is human to make mistakes and to err and the fact is the people here are very forgiving and very encouraging and I think whoever may have been responsible, accidentally, that people will accept that as well.

CONTINUED ON PAGE 2

17

9 771473 621009

DON'T FORGET
Next Week is
BLUE BIN WEEK

St Michael's Scout Band on their tour of New York in 1998

OFFICE OF THE PRESIDENT
BOROUGH OF QUEENS
CITY OF NEW YORK

PROCLAMATION

Greeting:

WHEREAS, in 1996 New York is commemorating the 150th anniversary of Irish Immigration with many programs and activities representing the rich contributions of the Irish people to America; and

WHEREAS, the St. Michael's Scout Brass Band Enniskillen Ireland, which consists of 81 talented young males and females, ages ten to twenty, is visiting New York this summer; and

WHEREAS, this Band, is recognized as one of the leading youth bands in Ireland, is traveling to America for the first time; and

WHEREAS, under the direction of Bernard O'Connor, the band will be performing throughout the City for the enjoyment of New Yorkers; and

WHEREAS, the Band will be performing at Fort Totten in Queens, as part of an event sponsored by the Bayside Historical Society

NOW, THEREFORE, I, CLAIRE SHULMAN, President of the Borough of Queens, in the City of New York, do hereby proclaim Thursday, July 18, 1996

ST. MICHAEL'S SCOUT BRASS BAND ENNISKILLEN IRELAND DAY

in Queens, in recognition of the special visit of this wonderful band to our borough, city and country.

Done at Queens Borough Hall, Kew Gardens, in the City of New York, on this the eighteenth day of July in the year one thousand nine hundred and ninety-six.

Claire Shulman

CLAIRE SHULMAN
President of the Borough of Queens

The 22 grandchildren of Bernard O'Connor

My two great grandsons, Rory and Eoin, aged five and eight

My one and only great granddaughter, Niamh, aged two

My daughter Aine and family with her husband, Dan, who was tragically killed in a road accident on St Stephen's Day 2014

The Silver Wolfhound, which is the highest Scouting award of the CBSI, presented to me in 2010

The US Medallion of honour, presented to me for my achievements with the Scout Band in the US

Andrew Lloyd Webber speaking with me at the premier of his Musical, 'The Beautiful Game' in London

With British Prime Minister Tony Blair, 2005

US Cl Tracy Nicholson, Commander at Fort Hamilton, presenting me with the Medallion of Honour

Mayor Juliani with US International Scout Commissioner, Gary Schiller and the Scout Band at the City Hall, New York

Roisin and me with Deputy Leader, the late Martin McGuinness

Roisin and my wedding, November 5th 2010

My son Brian with Ciara and their two sons, Daragh and Ruairi

My daughter Meabh with Marty and their four children, Aoife, Turlough, Clodagh and Erin

My son Philip with Helen and their four children, Michael, Mairead, Joe and Dan

My daughter Sinead with Andy and their family – Lucy, Claire and Cathal

My daughter Maire with her family – Odhran, James, Feidhlim, Seana and Domhnail

My daughter, Aine, with her four boys – Ciaran, Michael, Oisin and Eoin

My daughter, Nollaig

My daughter, Nuala

The grandchildren with their late Granny Pat

Roisin and me on holidays in Rome

Story Terrace